ENTER THE WHOLE ARMY

C. WALTER HODGES enjoys a unique reputation as illustrator and scholar of the Elizabethan theatre. This book consists of fifty of his drawings, with accompanying text, which together reconstruct the original staging of scenes from Shakespeare's plays. It offers imaginative solutions to the puzzling questions which surround those early performances at the large public and smaller private theatres.

Hodges' pictures are informed by a deep understanding of the theatre conditions of Shakespeare's time. Many of them have appeared in volumes of the *New Cambridge Shakespeare* edition. Together they provide a pictorial reconstruction of an Elizabethan playhouse such as the Globe, as well as less well-known indoor or private playhouses such as the Blackfriars.

Hodges creates visual explanations for specific incidents and bits of stage business in the plays: the different uses of the 'discovery space' and upper stage or gallery; the placing of beds and thrones; the creative use of stage posts and trap doors; the employment of special effects such as gunfire, or a god descending from Heaven. He provides solutions to the difficulty of staging, for example, Cleopatra's monument, the siege of Orleans, and, in the words of the title, how to represent a 'whole army' by a few actors.

This is an attractive and timely book. With the rebuilding of the Globe Theatre on Bankside, scholars, actors and directors are confronting again the problems of staging Shakespeare's plays. Walter Hodges' ingenious and practical solutions will appeal to students and theatregoers alike.

C. WALTER HODGES has, uniquely, combined a professional career as illustrator and graphic designer with the writing of scholarly books on Shakespeare's theatre, the latter featuring his own drawings. His books include *The Globe Restored* (1939), *Shakespeare's Theatre* (1964) and *Shakespeare's Second Globe* (1973). He has provided pictorial solutions to problems of staging in volumes of *The New Cambridge Shakespeare* since its inception in 1984.

ENTER
THE WHOLE ARMY

A PICTORIAL STUDY
OF SHAKESPEAREAN STAGING
1576–1616

•

C. WALTER HODGES

CAMBRIDGE
UNIVERSITY PRESS

PUBLISHED BY THE PRESS SYNDICATE OF THE UNIVERSITY OF CAMBRIDGE
The Pitt Building, Trumpington Street, Cambridge, United Kingdom

CAMBRIDGE UNIVERSITY PRESS
The Edinburgh Building, Cambridge CB2 2RU, UK
40 West 20th Street, New York NY 10011–4211, USA
477 Williamstown Road, Port Melbourne, VIC 3207, Australia
Ruiz de Alarcón 13, 28014 Madrid, Spain
Dock House, The Waterfront, Cape Town 8001, South Africa

http://www.cambridge.org

First published 1999
Reprinted 2000
First paperback edition 2004

Typeset in Monotype Ehrhardt 11/15pt, using QuarkXPress™ [SE]

A catalogue record for this book is available from the British Library

Library of Congress cataloguing in publication data

Hodges, C. Walter (Cyril Walter), 1909–
Enter the Whole Army: a pictorial study of Shakespearean staging, 1576–1616
/ C. Walter Hodges.
p. cm.
ISBN 0 521 32355 X hardback
1. Shakespeare, William, 1564–1616 – Stage history – To 1625 –
Pictorial works. 2. Shakespeare, William, 1564–1616 – Stage
history – England – London – Pictorial works. 3. Theater – England –
London – History – 16th century – Pictorial works. 4. Theater –
England – London – History – 17th century – Pictorial works.
I. Title.
PR3095.H59 1999
792.9′5–dc21 98–29341
CIP

ISBN 0 521 32355 X hardback
ISBN 0 521 31170 5 paperback

CONTENTS

ILLUSTRATIONS

The pictures in this book, excepting only those from historical sources in the first chapter, were all drawn to accompany the separate volumes of *The New Cambridge Shakespeare*, where they are intended as a guide for the reader in imagining the plays as they would have appeared in their original mode of performance on the stage of an Elizabethan or Jacobean theatre. Thus they should show at a glance the meaning of general stage-directions such as *Enter above . . .*, or of more particular ones such as (from *The Tempest*) *Here Prospero discovers Ferdinand and Miranda playing at Chess*, where 'discovers' means simply that he reveals them by drawing back a curtain. But when all my illustrations had been completed for those limited purposes it appeared to me that, seen together as a collection, they covered a broader subject than was at first intended. Collectively they form a comprehensive picture of the structure and management of the stage Shakespeare had worked with, at least as seen through the imagination of a modern reporter – for 'imaginative', to a great extent, any such report will have to be: without the support of imagination, the total of contemporary evidence, even – or perhaps especially – in the case of that most famous of all historic theatres, Shakespeare's Globe on Bankside, is scarcely enough for us to work with.

We are in fact fortunate in having any actual pictorial evidence at all. As is described in the first chapter here, it was only by chance that a Dutch visitor to London who happened to go into the Swan theatre one afternoon in 1596, happened also to have the knack for drawing sketches, and that he later took the trouble to write a description of the theatre, with a sketch of a performance on its stage which he sent home in a letter to a friend, who copied it, sketch and all, into a notebook which has by chance survived into our own time. Without that succession of simple chances we should have no knowledge at all of what the interior of any public theatre had looked like in the London of Shakespeare's day, and whatever we might have guessed about it would almost of a certainty have been wrong. Without that sketch, who would have imagined such a thing as a thrust-forward rectangle of a stage, with two great pillars standing upon it, more or less in the way of the actors, the vision of the audience, and everything that went on there? Yet that stage and those pillars have now established themselves firmly in theatre history as the characteristic, even emblematic background of Shakespeare's professional life. Nobody doubts them, and I have shown them as familiar features in my drawings throughout this study.

It should be noted here that the designs for the stage shown in my drawings, as well as many of the drawings themselves, were made over a period of several years before the unexpected discovery of the Rose theatre in the Spring of 1989. That excavation did not alter, but basically confirmed, many things that had been previously only conjectural. And it added some unexpectable details. For example, it confirmed what had often been supposed, that the theatre yard was set at a slight rake down towards the stage all round, but added the surprise that its surface was entirely composed of an aggregate of cinders and hazelnut shells. Of course, we need not go on to suppose that all theatre yards were surfaced in the same way, but so it was at the Rose.

I am aware that there are a few occasional inconsistencies in the stage details of my reconstructions between different drawings (though never, I hope, among any for the same play). Some of my stages have a low railing around their outside edge, others have not: the two posts are not always in quite the same position: the curtained opening in the back wall is sometimes set in line with the wall, with the curtains on their rail sometimes in front of the wall or at other times behind it; or sometimes it forms a structure of its own, built forward as a sort of porch. But I hope these and other differences of my stage layout, between one example and the next, may not be thought of as inconsistent lapses, but rather as what I might call 'exploratory variations'. I deliberately did not begin this series of pictures by first inventing a set of permanent fixtures, using the 'Wooden O' as a sort of Elizabethan half-timbered cage within which to bend the plays into suitable positions of historic conformity. In that way, if any layout should happen to be wrong in the beginning it would have to be wrong throughout, and one would miss even a chance of getting it right by mistake. Therefore I decided, in my representations of the Elizabethan stage, to allow myself a certain liberty with my interpretation of it, holding that if a drawing is to have success in suggesting a living reality, it ought at least to have a life of its own. I hope that, as illustrations, the drawings are convincing and appropriate, but as statements beyond that they should not be expected to be final or definitive solutions to outstanding and still unresolved problems. For an example of this we should look back once more to the thing I have so confidently described above as 'that thrust-forward rectangle of a stage'. At the beginning of this century, in a book entitled *The Shakespearean Stage*, Dr V. E. Albright published a drawing of 'A Typical Elizabethan Stage', showing it as thrust-forward into a round yard, not in the form of a rectangle, but wedge-shaped, tapering towards the front. In either a round yard, as that of the Globe, or a square one as of the Fortune, this is a workable plan, and indeed Dr Albright proposed it for both. It disagrees, however, with the powerful and over-riding evidence of the Swan drawing, and so, except for its appearance in earlier publications such as Ashley Thorndike's *Shakespearean Theatre* of 1916, it has disappeared from the scene. The rectangular stage still retains its dominance. Nevertheless when, after three hundred and forty years, the foundations of an actual Elizabethan theatre – the Rose – were discovered on Bankside, the shape of its stage was clearly seen. It was wedge-shaped, with its sides gently tapered towards the front.

I ought therefore to express a personal opinion at this point, though, to be less dogmatic, I will call it simply a preference. I think a taper-fronted stage is particularly suitable within a square-yarded theatre such as the Fortune. Given the known plan dimensions of the Fortune's auditorium and the supposed but rather less clear measures of its stage, I have always been puzzled by all reconstructions of it, which leave two narrow vacant gangway areas down each side of the stage at yard level, between that and the audience galleries. If, however, the stage were less wide at the front than at the back these embarrassing 'gangways' would be opened out to become useful and accessible parts of the main yard. It would be very sensible. With a round or polygonal yard it would also be sensible but not so decisively, because the side-spaces are not so narrowly proportioned from the yard itself. I therefore feel able to retain as a personal preference, a loyal liking for the rectangular stage which has become, perhaps because of its peculiarity, a favourite reconstructional tradition. To the objection that the Rose has now been shown and proved to be a round theatre with a tapering stage I can offer only one explanation: that the Rose was a very small theatre wherein the tapered stage allowed more elbow-room in a crowded yard. But I have to admit also that the argument enables me to retain my long-standing and habituated preference for rectangles.

For all my reference quotations from the plays I have used the 1953 edition of the Nonesuch Shakespeare which combines the complete First Folio text with all the Quarto variations in the margins: only I have occasionally modernised the spelling, thus (perhaps too puritanically) denying myself that pleasant but sentimental sense of historic 'local colour' given by the original.

My enthusiasm, with what may perhaps be described as my 'inventive researches' in this absorbing subject, has been spurred and guided by the works of a host of great scholars for whom I would like to think this book could be a modest token of the tribute I owe. It goes without saying that I have depended greatly upon the four volumes of Sir E. K. Chambers' *The Elizabethan Stage* of 1923, with its successors in G. E. Bentley's *The Jacobean and Caroline Stage*. I must also recognise my dept to T. W. Baldwin's *Organization and Personnel of the Shakespearean Company* of 1927, to A. C. Sprague's *Shakespeare and the Audience*, A. E. Thorndike's *Shakespeare's Theatre*, and to J. Cranford Adams' *The Globe Playhouse: Its Design and Equipment*, of 1942, and more recently to Herbert Berry's *Shakespeare's Playhouses.* I wish also to recognize the valuable help given by my son Crispin Hodges while preparing this work for the press. For the many others in a list which there is not space enough here to mention by name I can only hope they will not haunt me for my seeming neglect, though I fear they may. But there is one work which I must certainly not fail to acknowledge, for it engrossed and inspired me when I was a student and has remained as a colour in my memory ever since. It is Harley Granville-Barker's matchless series of *Prefaces to Shakespeare.* That must therefore be considered one of the origins of this book, to which I am hereby subscribing a preface of my own.

C. W. H.

1 The First Playhouse (the Theatre) 1576.

CHAPTER ONE

THE MALONE TRADITION

•

Among its first acts at the beginning of the English Civil War, the puritan Parliament in London issued an edict called *A First Ordinance Against Stage Plays and Interludes*; thus it abolished, as it hoped for ever, the whole profession of play-acting and all its works. It had been, in the view of that Parliament a notorious offender against public order and morality for half a century. The edict came into effect on 2 September 1642, and on that day the few 'playhouses' still working in London – they had all been feeling the pinch of the troubled times – finally shut their doors, became slowly derelict, and were eventually pulled down. The players disbanded their companies and went out to find what other employment they could. Some took service in the king's army and fought through the war: some were killed in it. Afterwards a few came together again and tried surreptitiously to put on a season of plays at a small theatre, a converted cockpit, which they found still standing; but at their third performance they were broken in upon by a company of soldiers and marched straight off the stage into prison, still in their stage clothes. That was the last scene ever played upon the stage of the great playhouse tradition that had survived from Shakespeare's time.

The Shakespearean theatre, which from its character and date of origin is usually allowed to be known as 'Elizabethan', even into the reign of James I and later, had thus come to an end after a continuous career of just sixty-six years. It had begun with the building of the first public playhouse, called The Theatre, in the London suburb of Shoreditch in 1576, and it ended with the Ordinance of 1642. Within that span it had been a phenomenon unsurpassed by anything in theatre history. There at that historic moment in London, for the first time anywhere, certain companies of common actors established themselves as an independent profession, with their own managers, their own writers, their own finances and, above all, their own specialised buildings where, at their own gates, they collected the entrance money from their own large and enthusiastic audiences. In that sixty-six years in and around the City of London there had been built at one time or another no less than sixteen permanent playhouses, a thing not equalled in any other city in the world for another two hundred years. Often there might have been five or six of these playhouses in work at the same time, and it was claimed that the largest of them could hold audiences of up to three thousand people. Considering the type of buildings they were, that was probably an exaggeration, but even so, from such information as we have it is likely that some of them were capable of cramming in at least two thousand. To try to estimate a total of great numbers of people, some standing, some seated, all moving about, with little to estimate from but common report, and with no standard method of checking the count, cannot be very reliable, but it is worth noting that the total of people who were the regular patrons of those London theatres in those sixty-six years may certainly be numbered in millions. It is therefore the more remarkable that when this prodigy was brought to its abrupt end in 1642, it all vanished like smoke. Of the theatres themselves, their stages, methods and traditions, nothing remained; and out of all those millions of witnesses, no-one in England, it seems had ever thought it worth while to describe any of them, or what it had been like to see a play there. Visitors from abroad, for whom the London theatres were an outstanding feature, like nothing to be seen in any other city in Europe, had occasionally written to friends about them in letters, some of which have survived. But for Londoners themselves to visit a playhouse was simply an everyday thing, nothing to write home about, nothing to put on record. They could not have known that these common buildings, during their brief time of popularity, had been unique. Their form, style and theatrical usage had been unlike anything of the sort ever seen before or since, and when they were abolished they disappeared completely. After the Restoration in 1660, when playgoing was resumed in London, it took place in other theatres, newly built and of an entirely different kind.

From the time of the old-style playhouses, however, there did remain a great legacy: hundreds of books of printed plays, headed by the collected works of Ben Jonson and William Shakespeare. As it happened, the style of Jonson's plays could transpose fairly easily into the mode of the new Restoration stage. Making only a little allowance for Jonson's censorious temperament, *Every Man In His Humour* and *The Silent Woman* could fairly easily share a stage with Congreve's *The Way Of The World* or Vanbrugh's *The Provoked Wife*, and it can be said that onward from this point the characteristic mainstream of English drama was marked out chiefly by Jonson, not by Shakespeare. Though the supremacy of Shakespeare's genius was never in doubt, the eighteenth-century scholars who were editing from the original hurriedly-printed, and sometimes confused texts (which often had not been seen through the press by their author) though such scholars may have been able to clarify his meanings in terms of literature, the outlines of his intended stagecraft were difficult for them to find, let alone understand. For example Dr Johnson, whose admiration for Shakespeare could not be doubted, and whose own edition of the plays was published in 1765, found it appropriate in his editorial Preface, to make some excuse for what he considered Shakespeare's laxity of proper dramatic construction. He attributed this to the 'barbarity' of the age the poet lived in. He notes that 'Shakespeare found the English stage in a state of the utmost rudeness', and that the public he wrote for was 'gross and dark'. Thus, Johnson supposed, Shakespeare as a dramatist was simply doing his best with a barbarous state of theatrical affairs. What else could he have thought? He was a close friend of David Garrick, familiar with the great Drury Lane theatre with its own traditions and all its sophisticated array of changeable painted scenery and the rest: what, then, was he to make of Shakespeare's staging arrangements as in Act 4 of *Antony and Cleopatra*, with its rapid succession of fifteen separate and differently located short scenes on one supposed battlefield? It must have seemed to him primitive in construction and impossible in practice. And what, even, of the whole construction of *Romeo and Juliet*? For all its enduring popularity, this play, as Shakespeare left it on the page, seems to contain such a maze of inconsistencies in the matter of its staging that even today it is rarely seen without some if not many alterations.

For Johnson, as for all the editors of Shakespeare in the eighteenth century, a principal difficulty, unconsciously with them, lay in the basic tradition of their scholarship, which was simply the study of literature. The theatre and its drama, from the classical world of Sophocles and Seneca onwards, had come down to them as literature. There was a long and continuous history of literature: but of the theatre, in its own terms, there was no history at all. A play put upon the stage was simply literature in another form, personified by actors. But such a view was now altogether too limited. What had become needful was a study of the methods used by actors to make their transition from the page to the stage effective: in other words, a history of the stage and staging itself. Such a study was now about to be made for the first time.

Edmund Malone, an Irish lawyer and scholar of literature, had come to London in 1777 to work with George Steevens in the preparation of a new edition of Shakespeare's plays. Steevens had earlier collaborated with Dr Johnson, and Malone himself presently became a member of the Johnson circle. It may have been through Garrick that Malone also became specially interested in theatrical technique as a subject in its own right, for it was at this time in his work on the new Shakespeare edition that he conceived the idea of an appendix to it, which would have the purpose of explaining certain puzzling elements in Shakespeare's stage directions, and of his dramaturgy in general. This led him back into theatrical folk history, and much more, and what had been started as an appendix rapidly outgrew that function and became a work on its own. Malone published it in 1780 as a volume separate from his Shakespeare, which he called *An Historical Account of the Rise and Progress of the English Stage*. In it Malone, having traced the English theatre from medieval times to 'the period of its maturity and greatest splendour' in the age of Shakespeare, then said he would 'endeavour to exhibit as accurate a delineation of the internal form and economy of our ancient theatres as the distance at which we stand and the obscurity of the subject will permit'. Here he included a picture of the old Globe playhouse on Bankside (fig. 3). It was his printer's woodcut made from a sketch specially copied for him by a clergyman friend in Cambridge, from the Bankside portion of C. J. Visscher's panorama of London

E. MALONE ESQ^r

Engraved by Bartolozzi from a Picture painted by Sir Jos.^a Reynolds.

London Printed for J. Bell British Library Strand May 16.th 1787.

2 Edmund Malone. Engraving by Bartolozzi, from a portrait by Sir Joshua Reynolds, 1787 (National Portrait Gallery).

HISTORICAL ACCOUNT 51

It was situated on the Bankside, (the southern side of the river Thames,) nearly opposite to Friday-street, Cheapside. It was an hexagonal wooden building, partly open to the weather, and partly thatched[2]. When Hentzner wrote, all the other theatres as well as this were composed of wood.

[2] In the long Antwerp View of London in the Pepysian Library at Cambridge, is a representation of the Globe theatre, from which a drawing was made by the Rev. Mr. Henley, and transmitted to Mr. Steevens. From that drawing this cut was made.

E 2   The

3 The Globe. Woodcut (after Visscher) from Malone's
Rise and Progress of the English Stage, 1780.

engraved in 1616. That print is now well-known, but was then of course a rarity. Malone's friend had found it in the Pepysian Library in Magdalene College. Visscher's Globe detail is quaint enough in itself (fig. 4), but Malone's woodcut is quainter, and it cannot have helped very much to correct Johnson's opinion of the old theatres as being in a 'state of the utmost rudeness'. Quaintness, though, was in those days a quality expected, and indeed enjoyed, in objects of antiquity, and it continued to haunt the rediscovery of the Globe theatre's real nature for all of the next hundred years.

Malone said he had been unable to ascertain when the Globe was built, but he believed (incorrectly) that it was 'not long before 1596'. Of the form of the building, he supposed it was 'hexagonal on the outside, but perhaps a rotunda within'. Thus he combined his woodcut version of a polygonal Globe with Shakespeare's famous reference to a theatre interior as a 'wooden O'. He then goes on to describe the Globe's characteristics and stage practices, so far as he could deduce them comparatively from play texts, in an account which remained in general use for over a hundred years, and which we may here call the Malone tradition.

First, he conjectured that the general arrangement of the Elizabethan public theatres had been derived from that of the inn-yards where the travelling players in former times, and still in Shakespeare's day, used to set up their stages: it was an open yard where the stage would be surrounded by a standing audience, the yard itself being closed round by the galleries which normally gave access to the upper rooms of the inn, but which during performances would also be thronged with spectators. He found that the stages were commonly fitted with curtains, though it was evidently not clear to him how or where. He stresses, however, that these curtains, wherever they were, were not drawn 'by lines or pulleys' which were 'an apparatus to which the simple mechanism of our ancient theatres had not arrived'. And then he says: 'towards the rear of the stage there appears to have been a balcony, the platform of which was probably eight or nine feet from the ground. I suppose it to have been supported by pillars . . . and in front of it curtains likewise were hung'. He then goes on to speak of scenery, taking several pages to explain to his readers, presumably to their surprise, that

4 The Globe playhouse. Detail from C. J. Visscher's etched panorama of London, 1616.

Shakespeare's theatre did not use any such thing. But, he says, 'the want of scenery seems to have been supplied by the simple expedient of writing the names of different places where the scene was laid during the progress of the play, on boards, which were disposed in such a manner as to be visible to the audience'. But 'though the apparatus for theatrical exhibitions was thus scanty, and the machinery of the simplest kind', Malone found evidence for the use of trap-doors on the Elizabethan stages, and that, above, 'the covering or internal roof of the stage was anciently called *the heavens*. It was probably painted of a sky-blue colour; or perhaps pieces of drapery tinged with blue were suspended across the stage . . .'

Then in 1780, while his *Rise and Progress of the English Stage* was still mint-new in the bookshops, Malone acquired an unexpected windfall. 'Some curious Manuscripts relative to the stage were found at Dulwich College' he wrote in a later edition, 'and were obligingly transmitted to me from thence'. 'Obligingly' is perhaps a mild word for the liberality with which the Master and Fellows of the College allowed Malone to carry the whole remarkable archive of the Henslowe/Alleyn papers back with him to his own study. 'I am unwilling' he then wrote 'that the publick should be deprived of the information and entertainment these very curious materials may afford, and therefore shall extract from them such notices as appear to be worthy of preservation'. He published his extracts in his next edition, in 1790. Among them were the builders' contracts for the Fortune and the Hope playhouses; an inventory of stage costumes belonging to the Lord Admiral's company of players in 1598, ('leaft above in the tier-house, in the cheest'); and a most fascinating list of the company's stage properties. (Malone's transcription of the list in his *Rise and Progress* is now its only source, for since his day the original has been lost.) Besides these were letters to Henslowe from playwrights and actors, mostly about advances of money, and above all Henslowe's so-called 'Diary', a memorandum book detailing his theatrical expenses and other transactions over a period of eleven years. Here were in fact the documentary raw materials of theatre history as never found before.

So from his original inspiration of commonsense Malone was now able to deduce that the dramatical part of Shakespeare's genius had been born not in a desperate struggle against the grain of a primitive set of old theatrical makeshifts, as Dr Johnson had seemed to suggest, but by making the fullest use of the new type of specialised, permanent playhouses, whose styles and techniques were being developed just at the time Shakespeare came to join them, and probably with his help. But, in any event Malone's inspiration at the end of the eighteenth century was itself only just in time to rescue the memory of those unique former playhouses from oblivion. They were already one hundred and fifty years away downstream when his *Rise and Progress* was first published, and we can see now that his retrieval of them in that first edition was by itself barely sufficient. The later discovery of the Alleyn/Henslowe archive at Dulwich, most likely because the keepers of the archive had seen his book, cannot have been other than a conclusive and fulfilling godsend. What was now opened up for future generations of scholars to continue, was to collate and analyse the whole body of Elizabethan and Jacobean dramatic texts, with a confident assumption that all together their stage directions, and the spoken references to action written into the dialogue, could be taken as representing a stable and methodical code of stage presentation, and not merely as a variable assortment of extempore local suggestions. With this in view, and with two editions of *The Rise and Progress of the English Stage* already to his credit, Edmond Malone had initiated the study of theatrical history itself, with Shakespeare's theatre at the heart of it.

In the last sentence above I had first written 'the *science* of theatrical history', but then cautiously changed 'science' to 'study' because of what follows. The whole subject of William Shakespeare and his theatre was now being embraced by the historical romanticism of the early nineteenth century, and I have to suppose that science and romanticism ought not to be so easily combined. Nevertheless in that prevailing romantic mode, the world of the Elizabethan theatre found itself easily at home. It was, and indeed still is for some, an island in the history of the imagination, closed around within a brief period of historic time, peopled with its coteries of actors, poets and courtiers, expressed in volumes of dramatic literature unlike anything before or since, and now as revealed by Malone and Henslowe, fed and held together by the common details of its daily life and business. It was in itself 'the quick forge and working-house of thought', sufficient for a lifetime, and, with the extra spur that certain parts of it are still hidden – the true nature, style, size and character of its different theatres, for example – is likely to remain so for at least a little while yet. The scientific study of Elizabethan theatrical history was begun not in England but in Germany. The prodigious writer, translator and admirer of Shakespeare, Ludwig Tieck, having already produced works on the Old English Theatre and on Shakespeare's predecessors, and now having a novel on that subject in his mind, in 1817 visited London to collect material inspiration for it. Malone had then been dead for five years, and his affairs had been left in the charge of his former assistant, James Boswell (the son of Samuel Johnson's biographer). Boswell must have acquainted him with the building contract of the Fortune Theatre, from the Dulwich archive, for Tieck copied and took all its details back with him to Germany. Some years later, when Tieck was in Dresden collaborating with A. W. Schlegel on their classic translation of Shakespeare into German, the idea occurred to them both that there in Dresden, on the banks of the Elbe, they might build, at full scale, a reconstruction of an *Altenglisches Theater* of Shakespeare's time, the Fortune, so that at last the great plays could be performed once again in their own proper style on a stage from their own time. In or around 1836, a famous architect, Gottfried Semper, had come to Dresden to build the Opera House there, and the two scholars persuaded him (or was it perhaps his own idea?) to prepare designs from the Fortune contract, whose details Tieck had brought with him from London.

It must be remembered that not anywhere among the surviving evidences of the public playhouses had there been found a single contemporary picture of an interior of any of them, nor anything to give a guide as to their architectural style or character, (I do not count for this purpose two very small details of actors on a stage, from the title-pages of plays printed in Caroline times, which could not have been useful on their own). The only idea in force was still Malone's, of a common derivation from the character of English inn-yards dating anywhere from the Middle Ages to Malone's eighteenth century. Semper knew nothing of that, and translated his Fortune into the German Renaissance style, to which it seems Tieck may have added a few instinctive theatrical notions of his own. Semper's designs

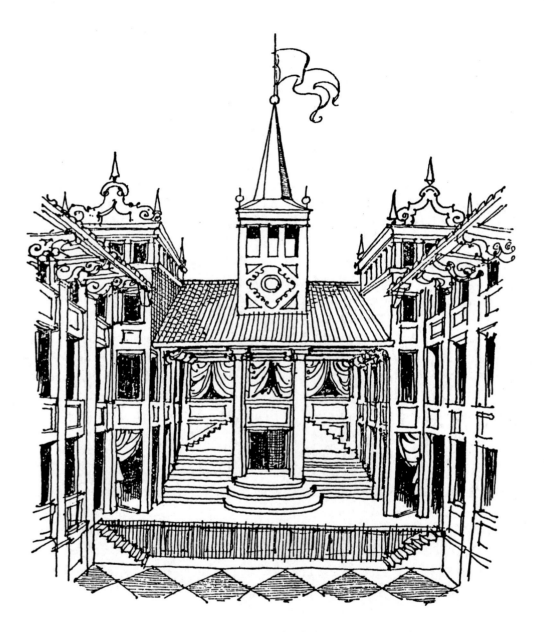

5 Design for a reconstruction of the Fortune Theatre by Ludwig Tieck, 1836.
(Pen and ink copy by the author from the original in the Munich Theater-Museum.)

– plans and elevations, and a watercolour view of the interior – survived in Dresden until they were destroyed in the air raids of the Second World War. (The illustration, a pen and ink sketch made by me from a photograph of Semper's interior view, though rather sketchy in some details, is generally reliable.)

The scheme was never carried out. One can guess it was hard to find backers for it. Tieck and Schlegel engrossed themselves again with their translations, and Semper with his Opera House. It was fifty years before another significant contribution was made in the recovery of the Shakespearean playhouses, and once again it came from Germany. Karl Theodore Gaedertz, a literary historian and librarian from Berlin, was searching among the documents of Dutch sixteenth-century humanists, in the library of the University of Utrecht, when he came upon a common-place book once kept by the scholar Arendt van Buchel (1565–1641), into which he had copied a letter from his friend Johannes de Witt. The letter had been sent from London, which de Witt was visiting in 1596. In it he describes his visit to the Swan playhouse which had been built the previous year, the newest and largest of the four playhouses then standing. De Witt's letter says it was reported as capable of holding three thousand spectators. He was especially impressed by its decoration, saying that the wooden columns that supported it were painted to resemble marble, 'so skilfully done as to deceive the closest inspection'. And on the same piece of paper as his letter he made a drawing, an actual sketch, at last, of the interior of one of London's unique public playhouses. Whether he drew it from his seat in one of the upper galleries of the theatre, and added the letter afterwards; or whether he drew it from memory, back in his lodging, where he wrote the letter (which incidentally was in Latin) we cannot know. But his friend van Buchel copied both the letter and the drawing carefully into his common-place book, which Karl Gaedertz had now opened and which lay there in front of him three hundred years after its time.

It is a drawing copied from a lost original: but how correctly drawn was that original, or how faithful the copyist? It is easy to see things in the copy which look 'unprofessional', but despite that it is still an authoritative state-ment in a firm hand. The subject was a very complicated one for either van

6 The Swan Playhouse. Contemporary sketch by Arendt van Buchel after Johannes de Witt.

Buchel or de Witt to draw, and it has been shown in a recent study[1] that both men were capable and practised draughtsmen. It is as trustworthy a document as any we may now hope for.

Gaedertz published the drawing in 1888 with two other of his essays, in a small volume whose German title I translate as *Towards an Understanding of the Old English Theatre*, and it has since very well justified its title. It was received with astonished satisfaction throughout the field of Shakespeare studies, though it may be said the satisfaction was not unmixed with a degree of muffled disappointment. It was a thing long hoped for, but it was not at all what had been expected. That expectation, however, has had to revise itself. In the one hundred years since it was first published it has held and confirmed its position as the central image around which any imagining of Shakespeare's stage must still be formed; other pictures may also be formed, perhaps even found, as time and study proceed, and take their places alongside; but the Swan drawing and its influence, for well or ill, cannot now be belittled. It is reproduced here rather larger than its original size to help it make that point.

---

1 See the essay *De Witt, van Buchel, the Swan and the Globe* by Johan Gerritson, published by the university of Oslo Institute of English Studies, 1986. My own paper *Van Buchel's Swan*, *Shakespeare Quarterly* (Winter 1988) may also be of interest.

CHAPTER TWO

ELEMENTS OF THE STAGE

·

At one point in the previous chapter I ventured to think that Shakespeare might himself have offered his opinion in the designing of the new stages, and the tiring-houses which were being framed up behind them in London's new permanent theatres. It was not altogether an idle notion, and I repeat it here simply to underline the element of enterprise and invention in the English theatre at the time when Shakespeare as a young man was actively involved in all of it. In the late fifteen-eighties, when the Rose was being built, he was already an established playwright: and a few years later he had joined the very successful Burbage company, the Chamberlain's Men, with whom he quickly became a shareholding partner. He had entered the theatre at just the time when the player companies were furnishing themselves with a luxury of professional aids and amenities they could never have enjoyed nor planned ahead for in their former peripatetic way of life. If it is true, as Malone conjectured, that they had customarily made use of whatever convenient building features they had found to hand at the local inns or wherever else their stages were set up, they could now borrow and standardise the best of these into a composed or adaptable background, which they and their writers could henceforth take for granted in the preparation of their plays. It would be surprising if, while they were about it, a valued and energetic writer could not have suggested the advantage of a window here or another door there, or a little more space in there at the back. The companies, while enlarging their scope and style, could now invest money on dressing their stages to suit the taste of the time and of the educated gentry who had become an important part of their audience. With all this there was created an entirely unique form of staging, which belonged to the Elizabethan theatre alone. Its great plays have since its own time been adapted into the style of every other form of the theatrical arts all over the world. But as itself, having flowered for hardly the space of one human lifetime, it withered away in a sudden change of climate. It was demolished and never restored. What came later to take its place was something very different. So the theatre Shakespeare knew and worked for remains unique in history, a singular phenomenon.

As a form of art it was composed out of three conventions, all derived from the original necessary techniques of the travelling play-companies. (It should perhaps be remembered here that this condition did not end with the founding of the London playhouses. Many companies continued to go out on the road, as, in times of plague in London, when the theatres were closed by law, they all had to do.) The first of their conventional techniques was indeed the most ancient of all dramatic forms, that of speaking in verse. Poetry itself has been defined as 'memorable speech'.[1] Dramatic verse is a compact expression of character and emotion, designed not only to have a memorable effect upon its hearers, but to be memorised easily by the speaker. Thus, with only the instrument of a trained voice, anyone, even young children, having learned their verses (as all professional actors, to this today, talk about 'their lines') could carry about in their heads their parts in elaborate stories, ready-made with complex emotions usually far beyond the actor's own experience. He might be able to add colour to it according to his skill; but even without that the verse could stand up by itself and work; and, above all, it was 'portable'.

The second convention was a set of guidelines for the posture and move-ment of actors or groups of actors upon the stage, quickly adaptable and mutually understood, to take the place of elaborate rehearsals. Techniques of 'production' as we understand that today, could scarcely have existed. A company would always have on hand a fairly wide repertoire of new and old plays, any of which might be called for at short notice, with very limited time for preparation; but so long as everyone understood the general guidelines of stage practice all would go well. However, with the establishment of

---

1 See the Introduction by W. H. Auden and John Garrett to their anthology *The Poet's Tongue* (London, G. Bell and Sons, 1935).

permanent theatres, their enlarged stages being backed with upper galleries and windows and sometimes in addition by a curtained-off 'place behind the stage' for the preparation of furniture or special effects, and with increasing room on the stage for the assembly of greater numbers of actors all together, the range of necessary working guidelines themselves had to become more elaborate and controlled. So a system of stage management began to evolve. The large open stage began to develop its own areas of greater or lesser dominance, and directional movements around or over it began to have special distinctions of their own. References to this sort of stage management may be found embalmed in the texts of all Elizabethan plays either directly as stage-directions, or implicitly in the dialogue, though in that case they are often difficult to interpret. 'Where's Potpan, that he helps not to take away?' is all that is needed to indicate the hurry and bustle of the Capulets' servants clearing away the banquet in *Romeo and Juliet*; but 'Look out o'the other side your monument', at a very dramatic moment in the last act of *Antony and Cleopatra*, is by itself impossible to understand, and even with an explanation is not indisputable. Such references to stage management are interwoven everywhere throughout the fabric of Shakespeare's plays, and they form a trail of clues which if properly followed should help us to unravel the working methods of his stagecraft, which until Malone's day, and even after, had baffled the imagination of his literary editors. Indeed it was not until the twentieth century, with the establishment of comparative theatrical history as an organised study in itself, separate from dramatic literature or the memoirs of old actors, that the material and historical perspective existed, by which it could be done. The attempt to do it, or at least to contribute something towards it, here and now, is the chief purpose of this book.

Of the three formative conventions of the Shakespearean theatre, the third and most outstanding is simply the physical form of the stage itself and the attached features of its tiring-house. It should be understood that all of this, especially the tiring-house and the details of its frontage on the stage, was entirely composed of useful acting areas put together to form an architectural unit. And here we should note another contribution of the twentieth century to these studies: we now have a widely developed knowledge of comparative art and cultural history in all its forms, both refined and popular, which previous generations had not the means to enjoy. In popular terms we can now visualise the frontage of a theatrical tiring-house as built and decorated in a robust vernacular style. Or, in a more refined mode we may liken a play by Shakespeare to a work in music; say, a kind of dramatic oratorio with the soloists as actors, or as an early baroque opera in the style of Monteverdi. Thus we may imagine the stage itself, and its surroundings, as a sort of grand baroque organ-case, composed of the music, the instrument and its frame, all together. So at this point we may pause to examine the principal features of which this 'organ-case' frame is composed, making up the usual requirements of a typical Shakespearean playhouse. I give them here not as a list, nor as in any particular theatre, but as a schematic diagram, at fig. 7. The items shown are all common, well-attested by reference to Elizabethan stage-literature, and mostly of frequent use.

Item 1 is simply the acting area, which may be a theatre stage, or the floor of a great hall in a mansion or a college; in either case the audience (2) will usually surround it on three sides, and some may find occasion to sit on the stage area itself. There has to be, close at hand, usually at the back (3) a closed-off tiring-house space, where the actors prepare themselves, having at least two doors (4) giving access to or from the stage. These doors have to be fairly large, to allow the passage of big items of furniture: the thrusting-out of beds (as shown here) is frequently referred to. (There may be more doors than two: the diagram indicates four as possible.) Perhaps the most characteristic feature of all, belonging in theatre history as a dramatic fixture to the Elizabethan theatres alone, is a permanent upper-stage (5) which is usually reached by stairs within the tiring-house, but sometimes (though not shown here) from the stage itself. Associated with this upper-stage are various windows (6), and there is evidence that these sometimes had curtains. Sometimes at the front of the upper-stage there would be a balustrade or handrail, and because privileged spectators frequently sat at this position to watch the play it is given the number (2), as for the audience below. Item 7 is a column or post, this one only symbolic of several which stood about the stage to support the galleries or the roof. (Two very large ones are shown in the de Witt/van Buchal drawing.) Item 8, a curtain, is shown here attached

7 Diagram of Elizabethan stage conditions (cf. numeration in the text).

to nothing because, although there must have been one (or a pair) its position is optional or disputable. Certainly the most likely place would be central, between the two main doors of the tiring-house front, where they would close a large opening sometimes referred to as a 'discovery', wherein prepared set-pieces could be revealed or thrust-forward onto the stage. (Behind such a curtain Ferdinand and Miranda in *The Tempest* are 'discovered' playing at chess.) Many examples of this curtained area and its use are shown in the drawings in this book. The numbers 9a and 9b represent trap openings in the stage allowing for the ever-popular effect of ghosts or devils coming up out of the earth: 9a is a grave-trap, as used for Ophelia's funeral in *Hamlet*. Lastly 10 represents in diagrammatic form the splendid effects of divinities coming down from The Heavens (above the roof over the stage) throned on painted clouds, to startle heroes on the stage and reward the expectations of the audience. It was a very popular effect, although, according to report, not much to Shakespeare's taste, and some of the scenes where from the texts it seems to occur in his plays – such as the scene of Hecate visiting the witches, in *Macbeth* (3. 5) – are thought to have been written in by another hand.

The items shown thus in my diagram have now to be brought together within the 'wooden O' frame of an Elizabethan playhouse. Until a few years ago it would have been reasonable, even proper, to name it as the Globe; but since 1989, when archaeologists from the Museum of London, digging on Bankside, discovered the actual foundations of the Rose theatre, and then partly of the Globe itself,[2] it may be better now not to be so specific with names. Many of the drawings in this book were made before the actualities on Bankside came to light, bringing new and unexpected facts. It would still have been reasonable, before then, to draw a 'typical' public playhouse and call it the Globe, with another similar one called the Rose; but now we know that these two theatres were very different from each other, in size alone if in no other way. Note, then, my drawings herein (figs. 8 and 9) for Shakespeare's dramatic trilogy of *King Henry VI*. I had reconstructed the

---

2 At the date of publication of this book both these excavations are awaiting funds for their continuance

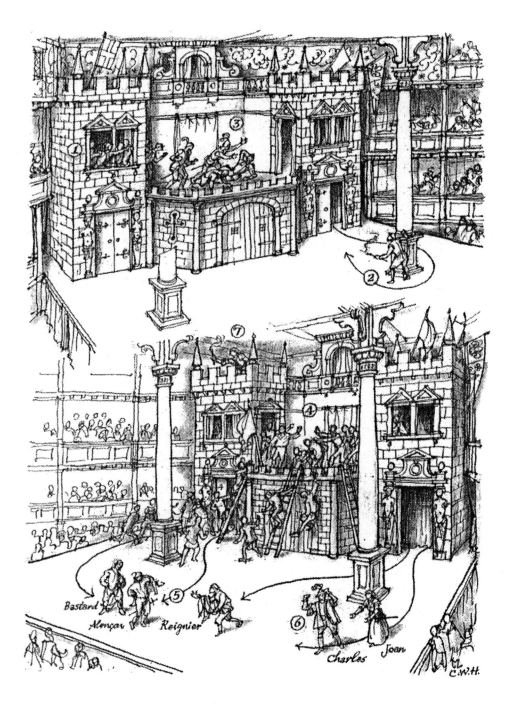

8 *The First Part of King Henry VI.* Conjectural staging for the scenes of the siege of Orleans, 1.5 and 2.1.

9 *The Third Part of King Henry VI*, 1.1.

staging of its first two parts for a theatre which I had designed conventionally as suitable for a 'typical playhouse', or the Globe if necessary (see fig. 8). Then, at that point, the Rose theatre was excavated, revealing the foundations of the very stage upon which one or more of the three Henry the Sixth plays had actually first been shown. It was in fact a small stage in a small theatre. So my next drawing, for the first scene of the third play of the trilogy, shown as upon a stage of the real proportions, may now be compared with the glamorous amplitude of my reconstructions for part one (fig. 9) and it gives rise to some sobering reflections. Nevertheless, though the glamour may be gone the principle of staging is the same, and I can claim that the difference illustrates a variability of resourceful treatment which was required in transporting a play from one playing-place to another. It should be remembered that most Elizabethan plays were thus transportable, as for example with Shakespeare's own company in their most successful days as the King's Men, in King James' time, moving between their indoor candlelit Blackfriars theatre, and their open-air daylit Globe, across the river.

Meanwhile, for reference, I reproduce here (fig. 10) my working diagram of a Shakespearean stage which may, if you will, be taken for the one at the Globe. I used it as a guide to maintain a general consistency in the drawings of staging which are to follow, although in most of these I have allowed it to take on a variety of different styles in decorative treatment. It is basically a conservative picture, taking its form, overall, from that established by the Swan drawing. Its dimensions are related to those of the Fortune Theatre, as given in the builder's contract. Its 'upper-stage' gallery, with its floor nine feet six inches above the lower stage, is within inches of Malone's own original conjecture. The row of windows in the gallery differ from those at the Swan only in that I have made nine of them instead of eight, and that they are round-headed. In the facade I have added four strong vertical posts to carry the main weight of the stage roof and the over-stage hut. Beyond that I have added a central opening onto the stage between the doors. As previously stated, most theatres seem to have been provided with something of the sort. The fact that the Swan does not show it is sometimes explained by the suggestion that when de Witt (the original 'sketcher' of the drawing) made his visit, the opening was somehow covered over and not seen by him.

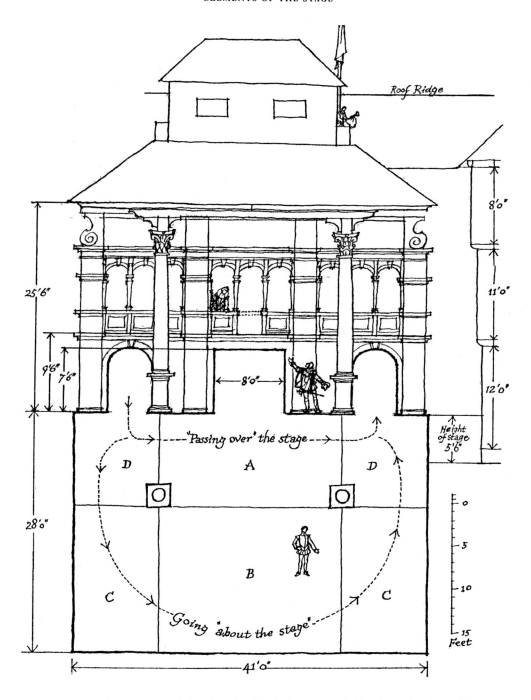

Roof Ridge

8'0"

11'0"

12'0"

25'6"

9'6"
7'6"

8'0"

Height
of stage
5'6"

"Passing over" the stage

D   A   D

B

C   C

Going "about the stage"

28'0"

41'0"

0
5
10
15
Feet

10 Scale diagram: plan and elevation of an Elizabethan stage and tiring-house (conjectural).

That may just be acceptable. What is not acceptable at all, however, is the featureless blankness of the whole main part of the facade as shown therein. In whatever way that was built, whether with infilled timber framing, or boards, or plaster, or canvas, it must somehow have been decorated, even if only painted all over with one flat colour; and if to that is added a second colour for door and window frames, a decorative scheme has already emerged; and beyond that, de Witt in his note with the Swan drawing states that parts of the theatre were painted to look like marble. I have taken that as licence to design the facade in a timber-framed 'classical' style, with turned posts between the windows, and mouldings and other details to give a modestly baroque flourish. The window at the centre of the gallery has a removable balustrade, making a walk-through opening for access to a front platform formed by the top of a small porch which, hung around with curtains, could give an additional facility to the 'place behind the stage'. This addition, which could be removable, is not shown in the diagram, but may be seen in some of the drawings hereafter.

The 'upper-stage' as shown in the diagram under discussion here is fronted, as was that of the Swan theatre, with a row of windows, as if suitable for an upper room (or rooms). Henslowe records money spent for attentions to 'the rome over the tyerhowsse'. This might of course be used by parties of gentlemen, as in the boxes of later-style theatres, or sometimes by musicians. A 'music room' is to be discussed in another chapter. But also to be discussed there is an entirely different style of the upper-stage as it was used in several theatres, especially in their earlier development: this was, as a wide and open acting area above and behind the main stage, not fronted by windows, nor even at all times by any railing or balustrade.

Also to be seen in a number of my drawings hereafter are suggestions of scenic painting, especially a traditional technique for representing the masonry of stone walls, as well as pillars painted on the flat, and some elaborate 'mannerist' ornamentation around the doorways, which I imagine was executed in a popular, painting-trade style.

To end these matters of style and practicality, a point should here be made about those two great posts standing out upon the stage, which first appeared with the publication of the Swan drawing, and have remained a significant feature of the image of an Elizabethan theatre ever since. Their authenticity has now been confirmed by the new evidence of the Rose excavation, where the bases of two such posts have been found not in the middle of the stage but actually at the forward edge of it. The posts are, of course, supporters for the stage roof and superstructure, but they raise a question of the spectators' view of the stage. What happens, for example, during a tense scene in a play, when an actor disappears momentarily from view, behind one of these obstructions? Together with this we have also to remember the auditorium galleries, which were fronted all the way round with supportive posts which must have blocked the sightlines from many of the gallery positions occupied by better-class patrons who had paid extra money for the comfort of a seat and a good view: what of that?

The question arises only because of our modern – or at least more recent – way of theatre-going, for which seats and sightlines are a primary consideration: and the answer is simpler than we may think. If an Elizabethan at a public playhouse found a post or pillar in his way, he simply moved himself along. We at a modern theatre buy at the box-office a numbered ticket for a seat in a fixed position in the house. The Elizabethan putting his money into the gatherer's box at the door, gained admission not to any single seat but to a whole area, where he might go as he pleased. If he arrived early he might choose himself a good general position and stay there. If he arrived later and the house was more crowded than expected he might find himself in the back parts of his gallery, with posts in his way. In that case he would very likely move about during the performance, standing a little, sitting a little, where he could. In the yard, where it was standing for everyone, all the time, he would doubtless move around a great deal, edging his way into more advantageous positions as other people themselves moved away. Of course for occasions of great success, with a very crowded theatre, this would be less possible. But it would rarely be not possible at all. We should imagine the whole audience at one of Shakespeare's plays at the Globe, always a little shifting, a little on the move, coming and going. But at those moments now and again when all was hushed and tense and there was no movement in the audience at all, those at last were the great moments they had paid for. That was why they went there.

CHAPTER THREE

SYSTEMS OF PRESENTATION

•

ROMEO AND JULIET; JULIUS CAESAR; THE MERCHANT OF VENICE; KING RICHARD II

The pre-eminence of the de Witt/van Buchel drawing of the Swan theatre as being the prevailing and only unchallengeable historical evidence for the appearance of the interior of an Elizabethan playhouse was emphasised here at the end of the first chapter. It would certainly surprise its authors if they could read the suggestion that with time it has become probably one of the most famous single drawings in the world: wherever the work of William Shakespeare is taught or printed in any language, that image of the Swan playhouse is likely to be found in attendance. Nevertheless its undoubted authority in theory is hedged about by questions which need to be answered in practice. The design for a composite stage, which is based upon it (fig. 10) has features which need to be explained; and even those two great stage posts, which by themselves seem to stand as the very emblem of the Elizabethan stage, ought to be questioned. Had they always stood there in all of the theatres, or for how long had they been such a dominant part of the scene?

In a book of essays[1] published to commemorate the four-hundredth anniversary of James Burbage's building of England's first playhouse, the Theatre, in 1576, Professor Glynne Wickham contributed a study of 'Heavens Machinery and Pillars in the Theatre and Other Early Playhouses'. In this he found that for all his careful reading of the documents relating specifically to the Theatre, these 'had failed to supply a single reference' to any roof structure or 'heavens' over the stage, 'or to stage pillars supporting

---

1 *The First Public Playhouse*, ed. Herbert Berry (Montreal, Queen's University Press, 1979).

them'; and then, searching through the whole body of relevant play texts for all the theatres then operating he found that 'they declare unanimously that no posts or pillars and no heavens machinery . . . are called for in any stage directions or dialogue before the building of the Rose began in 1587'. Wickham's deduction from this was itself supported by the twin pillars of commonsense and historical likelihood: peculiar architectural forms like that shown in the Swan drawing can hardly have sprung spontaneously into being from nowhere, without preliminaries. I therefore myself tried to visualise what an earlier form of playhouse, before the Swan, might have looked like, and I produced the series of sketches which is given here at (fig. 20). It shows the well-attested 'wooden O' circle of galleries with its 'tiring-house' conceived as a separate structure built into it, simply omitting the stage-roof superstructure. The 'battlements' and other ornamental features which I added above in its place are in a characteristic style of the time; but without these it will be seen that the tiring-house facade differs little if at all from that the Swan; and so this general picture may perhaps be accepted, for want of other evidence at present, as a precursor of it.

Professor Wickham's hypothesis about the pillars was proved correct in a most spectacular manner, when the foundations of the Rose were excavated in 1989. It was then found that the Rose had in fact been built twice, or, more correctly, in two phases. In its initial phase, of 1587, it had been, for a theatre, quite a small building; but in the second phase of 1592 its entire northern half was dismantled and rebuilt on a wider foundation. It may be presumed that The Heavens superstructure with its supporting pillars was added at this time. The excavation discovered the foundations of two separate stages, the first of 1587 being without posts, but the second of 1592 showing the positions of two posts, with their square bases clearly defined.

It was at this time that William Shakespeare, then in his late twenties, was in London working in the theatres. The legend about his lowly beginnings minding the horses of gentlemen who were inside the theatre at the plays was a popular story in the eighteenth century, but it was properly dismissed by Malone as 'altogether unworthy of belief'. Malone supposed instead that he was employed among the actors from the beginning, possibly starting as a prompter's assistant. Be that as it may, we find him first in 1592 making a name for himself in the newly established theatre district of Bankside with his plays of *King Henry the Sixth* and *Titus Andronicus*. The staging of these plays will be discussed later in another context. Meanwhile Shakespeare himself was changing his circumstances. He had hitherto been a convenient workaday playwright, employed by the actors to provide them with dramatic meat for their popular style of blood-and-thunder play-acting. But in the years between 1593 and 1596 he became a shareholding member of the Lord Chamberlain's Men, as their resident or 'ordinary' poet. With them he now developed that extraordinary quality as a dramatist which quickly helped them to become the most distinguished theatrical company in the land. The plays *King Richard II* and *Romeo and Juliet* were both first presented by the Chamberlain's Men at around this time.

KING RICHARD II

Shakespeare joined the Chamberlain's company while they were still working at the old Theatre in Shoreditch, but in 1596 they were in dispute with their landlord over a renewal of the ground-lease, and so they had moved out temporarily into the newly-built Swan playhouse on Bankside. It has been proposed by Andrew Gurr[2] that *Richard II* may actually have been performed on the stage of the Swan, the very stage that we see in van Buchel's drawing, and if so it would be proper to study its presentation under those conditions. My reconstruction drawing of 1.3 (fig. 11) may therefore be compared with the Swan sketch itself (fig. 6) on p. 14, where it will be seen that, apart from some decorative painting and some stage properties, nothing has been added nor taken away. As Gurr has said, there is nothing in the play which could not have been accommodated at the Swan as it is shown, and what is shown has no sign of any central opening or curtained recess between the two large doors. Such an opening is generally supposed to have been a necessity for all Elizabethan staging, and I show it thus in fig. 31. However, even without that convenience it is true that in *Richard II* there are no situations, nor any properties to be brought on, not

2 *King Richard II*, ed. Andrew Gurr (Cambridge Unversity Press, *The New Cambridge Shakespeare*, 1984). p. 35.

11 *King Richard II*, 1.3. The lists at Coventry.

even the royal throne of England itself, which could not be managed by either of the two doors. Yet here we should pause: this throne is the central feature and subject of the entire play, which it dominates throughout. To turn it into a mere property, hauled or toted in and out when needed, would be significantly to belittle it. I do not think this is a modernist idea based on modern visual modes of production, but to the contrary an essentially Elizabethan one. Moreover, the throne seems indicated in the dialogue as being set at some height above stage level. In my drawing at fig. 11 we are supposed to be viewing the tournament lists at Coventry, in 1. 3. The two contestants, Mowbray and Bullingbrook, whose interrupted combat is the spring that sets the play in motion, are in their 'chairs', armed and ready to be called into the lists. These 'chairs' as Professor Gurr explains are a customary name for the pavilions where the knights await their call to combat. Here on the stage the combatants are likely to have been placed one each at the foot of the two posts, as I show them. The king at a tournament would normally have been seated in a gallery overlooking the lists, but here he is seated high on his throne. That it was high in fact as well as in metaphor is apparent from the text at this point. Bullingbrook, before, going into the lists, asks leave to kiss the king's hand, 'and bow my knee before his majesty'. The Marshal in charge of the tournament ceremonial formally conveys this message to King Richard, who then says: 'We will descend and fold him in our arms'. This may of course be taken simply as a figure of speech: to rise from a throne and come down one step only might, in regal terms, be considered a descent: but 'we will descend' hardly sounds like that, especially as at a tournament a royal person would normally be seated in a high place. Then, soon after, when the king prevents the fight by throwing his staff of office into the lists, the Marshal cries out 'Stay, the King hath thrown his warder down', which in the real event would have been from a height, and on the stage must at least have simulated that. Later still there is more to suggest that this royal throne was set at a noticeable height above the stage. In 4. 1, the King having been defeated and taken prisoner, Bullingbrook is called upon by his followers to 'ascend the throne' in his place, 'and long live Henry, of that name the fourth'. Bullingbrook then says: 'In God's name I'll ascend the regal throne.' He does not at this time do so, however, for he is prevented by the Bishop of Carlisle with 'Marry God forbid!' and a long declamation about the evils that will come upon the land from such an overthrow of the true lineage. Meanwhile the tableau on the stage has the throne at its centre, with the Bishop on one side and Bullingbrook on the other, with his foot on the lowest step, but ascending no further.

The throne has stood thus at the summit of its pyramid of steps throughout the afternoon, and the action of the play has taken place all round it. Such an arrangement would have been in keeping with medieval tradition, where such pieces of furniture would wait on the stage in full view until their time of use came round; and in this case, as stated earlier, the throne would have exerted a certain symbolic value throughout. Perhaps for the purpose of illustration I have here drawn it larger than it needed to be: I might have made it two steps lower, and thus less obtrusive. Had there been at the Swan that central opening between the two doors (which the de Witt/van Buchel drawing does not show), there would have been little difficulty with rolling the throne, dais and all, on and off the stage as required; but it has been the purpose of this essay to show how it might have been done there without such an opening.

It may be remembered that at about this time the Chamberlain's Men had in hand another play by Shakespeare, *The Tragedy of Romeo and Juliet*, and it is certain that however they might have managed their *Richard II* at the Swan, without the facility of a central opening and its curtain, they could never have done the same with *Romeo and Juliet*.

It is likely that after a short stay at the Swan the Chamberlain's company transferred to an old playhouse, the Curtain, which had been refurbished for them in the meanwhile. They stayed there until their own Globe theatre was built and ready for them on Bankside in 1599. *Romeo and Juliet* was therefore probably first staged at the Curtain.

ROMEO AND JULIET

There is no record of when this play was first performed, but it was first printed in 1597 – in a 'bad' or unauthorised Quarto edition – with the title-page announcement that 'it hath been often (with great applause) plaid publiquely by the right Honourable the Lord Hunsdon his Servants'. (The

Chamberlain's company had, for technical reasons, been called Lord Hunsdon's for a few months only, during the winter of 1596–7). Apart from all its other qualities, one underlying reason for the great popularity of this play in its own time may well have been the remarkable skill and elegance of Shakespeare's stagecraft in it, with his adroit, even innovative use of all the systems of the Elizabethan stage. (For my attempt to illustrate this here it may be useful for the reader to mark the place of my stage diagram fig. 10 on p. 25).

I will begin at the end of Act 1, Scene 4. There is to be a ball at the house of the rich Capulet family. Romeo with his friends Mercutio and Benvolio and others of the (unwelcome) Montague clan are on their way to visit it, as 'maskers'. It was a hospitable custom for masked and costumed 'uninvited guests' to arrive at a celebration of this kind and be welcomed. So, costumed as pilgrims, led by a drummer and lit on the way by their several torch-bearers, Romeo and his friends are assembled, let us say, in the diagram areas B and C on the right-hand side. In the original texts, where the play is not divided into acts and scenes, when their little procession is ready to move off Benvolio simply says 'Strike drum', and the text then gives a stage direc-tions: *They march about the Stage, and Servingmen come forth with their napkins.* It must be understood that this 'march about' is not a random wan-dering movement but a precise direction, as in going 'around'. I show this going 'about' in my stage diagram as a rather broad sweep, but it might also be imagined as a straight pathway all around the margins of the stage, enter-ing at one door and going out at the other, and it seems to have been a well-established convention for a processional movement or a march. (We shall meet with it again in *Julius Caesar*). In the present instance the maskers with their drum and their torches have formed up downstage and march across and upstage to the door at D, and at the same time the curtains of the central opening part, and the serving men come hurrying out with their napkins, ('Away with the joint-stools, remove the court cupboard, look to the plate') and the whole stage is alive with a different scene, the great hall of the Capulet mansion. I think the procession of maskers will have gone off-stage at D, to re-enter at the opposite door a minute later. Meanwhile the servants have drawn the curtains fully aside for the entry, at centre, of old Capulet

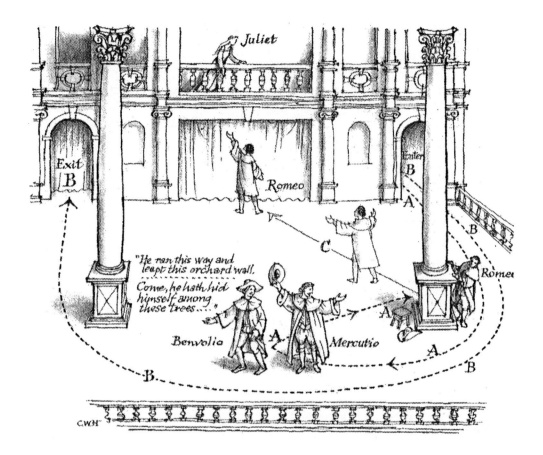

12 *Romeo and Juliet*, 2.1. The stage as pathway, orchard and window.

and his guests and gentlewomen, probably as couples for dancing, who come forward down the centre, led by old Capulet himself. Romeo and the other maskers and their torchbearers have now re-entered by the right-hand door upstage, and have completed their processional circuit about the stage down to the front at its centre, where old Capulet greets them with 'welcome, gentlemen:' and so the scene begins, where Romeo is to meet Juliet for the first time. There has been no break in the movement of the play, though the scene has all been changed by the bustling activity of its conventions.

With the opening of Act 2 these conventions are resumed at once, and with more to follow. The Capulets' ball is over, and we are to imagine that the pathway 'going about' the stage is now a lane outside the wall of the Capulet orchard (fig. 12). Romeo enters alone by the right-hand door, and comes forward, as we see in the drawing. Bemused by his love for Juliet, he has left his friends and finds himself, as we begin to learn (there are no stage directions to tell us what we later hear in the dialogue) on the outside of a 'wall' which is one of the more famous perplexities of Elizabethan stagecraft. Romeo hears Benvolio and Mercutio calling his name. He has run ahead of them. They enter following him, but cannot find him. 'He ran this way', says Benvolio, 'and leapt this orchard wall. Call good Mercutio.' There then follow thirty-eight lines of dialogue wherein they taunt Romeo with bawdy talk about his mistress, knowing him to be there, on the other side of a wall, though they supposedly cannot see him as we can. The situation showing both sides of the non-existent wall is shown in my drawing. I have supposed that Romeo, to be out of sight of his friends, is hiding behind one of the two stage pillars. I think it would have been proper for him to have simulated a climb in some way. Juliet later says that 'the orchard walls are high and hard to climb', and Romeo answers that 'Love's light wings' had helped him over. I have suggested that in fact he might have climbed up onto the plinth of the pillar and jumped down from it, and that this modest climb might have been assisted for stage purposes by a carefully positioned stool set ready for him earlier. I have even suggested that in his climb he has dropped his masquerade pilgrim's hat on the ground, and that Mercutio has caught sight of it there, and thus that he and Benvolio had known that Romeo was indeed hiding from them on the other side of the 'wall'; but that of course is a detail

beyond anything we need to conjecture here. Neither, I think, need we conjecture anything special to resemble the wall. Romeo is in hiding, actually
behind a pillar, but Mercutio and Benvolio have agreed with him that it is a
wall, and leave him there. ("Tis vain to seek him that means not to be
found'.) So with their exit the scene has changed again, and Romeo, moving
to the middle of the stage, is now in the orchard beneath Juliet's window.

Beyond this smoothly imagined change of scene there are in this play two
examples of a variation which we might describe as 'transposition'. A single
event supposed to be happening in one place is divided, and continued for
convenience in a quite different part of the stage. A clear example of this is in
Act 3, where Juliet, now secretly married to Romeo, is parting from him at
her bedchamber window which is on the upper level of the stage. She
watches him descend to the stage below by a rope ladder, which she then
draws up to hide away. At this moment her Nurse enters to warn her:
'Madam, beware, take heed, the day is broke / your Mother's coming to
your chamber, make all sure'. I quote those words from the First Quarto
version, which is unauthorised, and has sometimes been thought to have
been compiled from memory by actors who had originally taken part in the
play. The dialogue therefore has certain errors and omissions probably due
to faults of memory, but the stage directions are of particular interest
because the actors, though they may have forgotten some of their lines,
could well remember what had actually been *done*. So here, at the point
where Juliet, at her window on the upper stage, is warned of her mother's
approach, we have the stage direction: *She goeth down from the window*. This
she does by way of the stairs within the tiring-house, while her mother and
the Nurse come out onto the main stage below and cover her brief absence
by calling for her. Juliet then enters to them, and the scene continues as if it
were still all in the room above. The bedchamber has simply been 'trans-
posed'. A second example of this method will come into place later.

The stage directions in the First Quarto now provide us with direct evidence for that curtained central opening between the two doors, which we
found to have been lacking at the Swan. Juliet is alone on the stage preparing
to drink the potion which will bring on the death-resembling sleep from
which she is supposed to awake in Romeo's arms. She brings herself to drink

it and then, says the Quarto direction: *She falls upon her bed within the curtains*. It is evident that the curtains are closed completely, and that they hide her. There is then a brief scene on the stage with the family and servants making ready for the wedding feast. When they have gone the Nurse enters, as if again in the bedroom, to call Juliet. The silence of the closed curtains as the Nurse bustles about calling her, but not yet looking within, itself becomes increasingly tense until she at last opens the curtains and Juliet is discovered on the bed.[3] There follows a scene of family grief for her supposed death, and then the stage direction: *They all but the Nurse go forth, casting rosemary upon her and shutting the curtains*.

The series of conventional stage systems by which this play has been presented from the beginning now moves to its climax in Act 5, where all the conventions are elaborately woven together. The stage has now become a cemetery, with the family tomb of the Capulets. For my drawing in fig. 13 it will be seen I have supposed that the men from the tiring-house have come out in an interval between the scenes to dress the stage in a suitable and simple way. (Whether this would in fact have been done, or to what extent, is, I suppose, disputable; but what I show – the mournful garlands and the inscription over the tomb – would have been quick and easy, and is wholly in keeping with Elizabethan decorative practice.) The scene opens with the entry onto the stage of the young nobleman Paris, who was to have married Juliet, accompanied by his page, who carries a torch, thus signifying (for their audience in the afternoon) that on the stage it is night. Paris bids the page put out the torch ('for I would not be seen') and sends him to keep watch, and warn him if he hears anyone coming. ('Lie thee all along under this yew tree, keeping thine ear close to the hollow ground'). It is clear from everything that follows that the boy does not leave the stage, and that the 'yew tree' he lies down under is one of the two stage posts. A little later on the other post, also supposed to be a tree, is called into a similar service. (The effect of this action should here be visualised. A figure lying still on the ground beside one of these posts is in effect neutralised, out of the scene, and *visually* not in the way of whatever else is happening on the stage.)

3 A 'discovery' was a usual theatrical term for these stage curtains and the space behind them.

Paris has come to the churchyard carrying flowers to strew upon Juliet's tomb, and it is clear, therefore, that if the flowers are to be strewed on it, the 'tomb' must be low upon the ground. Paris says: 'Sweet flower, with flowers I strew thy bridal bed'. But at this point the strewing is interrupted. The page, with his ear to the ground under his 'yew tree', has heard footsteps approaching, and gives warning. (*Whistle Boy*, says the original stage direction). Paris withdraws and conceals himself, possibly with the boy behind the yew tree, or else back in the doorway by which he came in.

Romeo now enters, with his serving man Balthasar. They, also, have a torch with them, and also *a mattock and a crow of iron*. Romeo, not knowing that Juliet's death is only a simulation, is secretly intending to kill himself and lie beside her. He therefore bids Balthasar to leave him, but the latter, though he stands *all aloof* as instructed, is given no *exit* in the text, and it becomes evident that, like Paris' page, he lies down under a tree – i.e., the other stage post ('As I did sleep under this yew tree here . . .' as he afterwards explains). So now, with Balthasar and Paris' page both out of the way, each at the foot of his tree, and Paris himself concealed, Romeo prepares to open the tomb and, as he says, to 'descend into this bed of death'.

It is now necessary to consider the matter of this tomb, which in all productions of *Romeo and Juliet* since the disappearance of the original Elizabethan theatres has loomed up ahead as an obstacle impossible to overcome except by some sort of adaptation, alteration or cunning scenic subterfuge.

In order to arrive at a proper Elizabethan solution it would be useful if we could find out, or even only guess, what Shakespeare himself had in mind. We know that his direct source for the play was a long narrative poem by one Arthur Brooke, entitled *The Tragicall Historye of Romeus and Juliet*, published in 1562. Shakespeare followed the poem closely, and we may suppose that he had it with him on his work table. In the poem Romeus, like Romeo, dismisses his manservant, who 'Obediently a little withdrew himself apart,/ And then our Romeus, the vault stone set upright/ Descended down . . .' Coupled with Paris' 'strewing' of the flowers, this leaves little room for doubt that the tomb into which Romeo is to 'descend' must be set low or level with the ground and that its stone slab is prised open

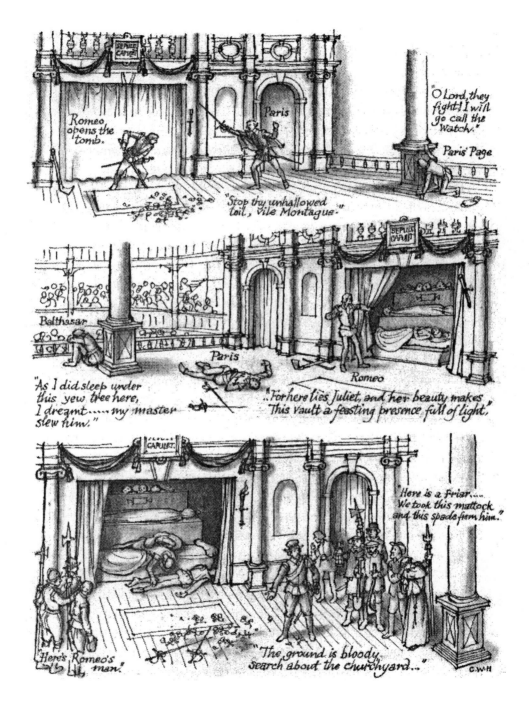

13 *Romeo and Juliet.* The stage as cemetery and tomb.

to stand upright. There is, we know, a grave-trap in the stage (it is much used: Ophelia's grave in *Hamlet* is an example), and we may suppose that Romeo will make use of this opening now. He has with him his mattock for clearing the ground, and his crowbar for prising things open, and he sets about his work with feverish energy: 'Thou detestable maw, thou womb of death. . . . Thus I enforce thy rotten jaws to open.' But before he can open them he is interrupted by Paris. It is in fact a critical moment not only in the play but in the stagecraft of it.

My drawing of this scene in fig. 13 (p. 40) may serve instead of much writing. I have supposed here that Paris had concealed himself not behind the post but within the stage door. I have for illustrational purposes shown Romeo as actually prising up the trap, but he needs not to do so in fact: simply for him to set to work on the job might be enough, though Paris has a few lines to speak before he comes onto the scene to challenge Romeo. The page then runs away as the duel begins. It is clear that for practical purposes the trap cannot have been opened, for the fight to come, however brief, would certainly be energetic and require a safe and clear space over the stage. So Paris is slain, and with his last breath begs Romeo to lay him (where Romeo had intended himself to be) beside Juliet in the tomb. Which Romeo will do: but how? In the *Romeus* source-poem there is a 'vault stone set upright', and Romeus descending. To 'descend' had been Romeo's intention. But how, now, carrying Paris' body with him? It would not be practicable. And yet the audience certainly has now to witness all the end of the tragedy being enacted not only outside but also *within* the tomb.

For Shakespeare the problem could be solved immediately by two quick paces over the stage and the use of that same 'transposition effect' that had earlier brought Juliet's bedchamber downstairs in Act 3. Romeo has only to cross the stage and draw back the curtains, and there lies Juliet on her death/bridal bed, just as we last saw her when her mourning family closed the curtains on her in Act 4. Remember, there has been a violent sword-fight, with the death of Paris, between the two systems of the scene; Romeo can now easily draw Paris's body into the tomb to lie with Juliet, the sense of the scene will be continuous and the transposition will be scarcely noticed, if at all. The join has simply been stagecrafted over.

41

The play then finishes operatically with a sort of coda or grand finale around the open tomb and the bodies of the tragic lovers. Paris' page comes back bringing in the Watch. The Watch lays hands on everybody needed to tie up loose ends, including Romeo's man Balthasar who has been I know not where during the last part of the play. He can hardly have been asleep under his tree during all of the fight between Romeo and Paris, although he seems to claim that he was. Perhaps the Watchmen catch him trying to sneak away. In any case he is back on stage with everybody else for the final homily by the Prince of Verona, during which the curtains will be closed for the last time over the sad tableau in the tomb.

Of my sequential drawing in fig. 13 I have to say that it is a little while since I drew it, and I rather repent me now of my 'scenic' rendering within the tomb, with the skulls, and Tybalt in his shroud, and all that. Of course the tiring-house people could easily have done it so, but it is doubtful whether they would have taken that trouble, or needed to; and I now myself think it would have been better without it.

JULIUS CAESAR

The stagecraft in *Julius Caesar* is generally less complex than that of *Romeo and Juliet*, but it follows the same well-understood conventions of concerted movement. Its formal, spectacular episodes are concerned with processions or the march of armies, and make strong use of the imagined roadway system going 'about the stage'. Contrasted with this are scenes of rabble and riot, which are differently described. The holidaying Commoners, with whose entry the play begins, are given as entering 'over the stage', a different movement (see fig. 14) which suggests they all enter at one door and spill out towards the middle of the stage where they are confronted by the prim authority of the two tribunes, who have entered by the other door. ('Hence: home, you idle creatures, get you home.')

There is little if any need in this play for a curtained central opening, or 'discovery space', between the two doors, and indeed, in my proposition here, there is no room for it. Its place is taken by the Pulpit from which in Act 3 Mark Antony will make his oration (fig. 15). This has to be a firmly-built structure of commanding height. Both Brutus and Antony have to go up

42

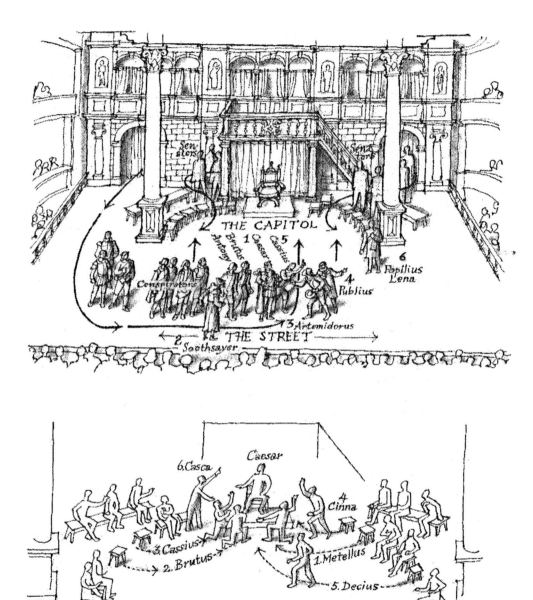

14 *Julius Caesar*, 3.1. The Capitol and the conspirators

into it and descend again, to make their speeches, and it surely must not shake unfirmly or the whole crisis of the play shakes with it. It has to be built and in position before the play begins, and remain so till it is over. I hope it may be agreed from my other two sketches (figs. 14 and 16) that it can thus be absorbed into the general scene without difficulty. Indeed, since it is already there it is later on made use of: in Act 5 it becomes a hill upon which first Cassius and afterwards Pindarus mount up to view the battle of Philippi. The frame of this 'pulpit', usually without its stairs, may be seen in some other of my drawings herein, as a thrust-forward addition to the main upper stage. It can be dressed in various ways or hung with curtains – as here, stairs and all – and is of so much use that I cannot think the Elizabethan stage would or could ever have done without it. Certainly there is no question about it being on stage here, as the Pulpit in the Roman Forum, for Caesar's obsequies.

It will be noted that for Antony's oration I have supposed the great crowd of the people of Rome is made up chiefly by the whole playhouse audience itself. The crowd on the stage has to be managed to help that illusion by spreading itself about, yet not obstructing the sight of Caesar's body. Including Antony, I have drawn twenty-three figures on the stage. It would call heavily upon the resources of the company and its backstage staff and helpers to provide so many, especially as some – Brutus and Cassius, for example – cannot be there at this time; and the stage is very large, which does not help. But Shakespeare deals with this difficulty by actually personifying so many people in the crowd that our attention is always on the move among them, continually refilling the empty spaces.

The two other scenes I have pictured may here be briefly described with references to fig. 14. In 3.1 the stage has been arranged to show the Capitol (Caesar's chair of state on a dais, thrust forward from the curtains at the back, and a semicircle of seats – ordinary stools for general use on the stage – quickly arranged for the Senate) and the street approaching it (going 'about the stage' as in fig. 10). The Grand Entry is announced by a Flourish of trumpets from the windows above, which probably would continue until the procession has arrived downstage. Then, when all the principals are at the front of the stage, the following exchanges take place, which I have

44

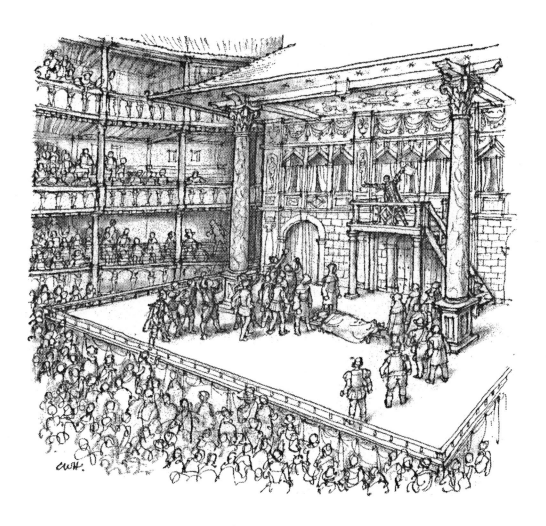

15 *Julius Caesar*. The 'pulpit' and Antony's oration.

marked with successive numbers on the drawing: Caesar (1) as he passes the Soothsayer (2) turns to him to say 'The Ides of March are come', which is followed by the Soothsayer's ominous 'Ay, Caesar, but not gone'. Then Artemidorus (3) attempts repeatedly to give Caesar his urgent letter of warning, but is prevented by Publius (4) with 'Sirra, give place', and Cassius (5), who says 'What, urge you your petitions in the street? Come to the Capitol'. At that point the procession turns and moves upstage into the Capitol area. One last exchange remains, with Popilius Lena (6). He has been waiting by the stage pillar on the right, and as Cassius passes, going upstage, he catches him by the sleeve with his sinister: 'I hope your enterprise today may thrive'. Cassius takes alarm, and Popilius moves away. Brutus and Cassius now hang back, with anxiety, while the rest move on to their places in the Capitol. ('What said Popilius Lena' . . . 'I fear our purpose is discovered' 'Look how he makes to Caesar', etc). There is a hurried conference showing their alarm which is joined by Casca, at the centre front of the stage, while all the rest are taking their places upstage; and the three conspirators now hurry to join them. (Here I notice that my drawing shows other 'Senators' moving into the scene from behind in the tiring-house, to swell the numbers in the Capitol. I think now I should revise that. Surely any other persons available for duty as Senators would have followed in the procession.)

In the lower sketch I have suggested a sequence, with numbers, showing how the conspirators have taken their places in the Senate, and how they then move forward for Caesar's assassination. Having started the scene I felt a need to complete it.

My next example (fig. 16) shows the same system of staging in use for Act 4. The scene here opens with the sound of a drum, and then Brutus enters with his army. He marches down the 'roadway' from the upstage door and halts downstage right. Then we hear distant drums approaching (stage direction: *Low march within*) and *Enter Cassius and his Powers* from the other door, marching to downstage left. Both armies now being halted Brutus and Cassius move to meet each other downstage centre. There then begins the famous Quarrel Scene, or Tent Scene, as it is variously called ('Most noble brother, you have done me wrong'). There certainly is a quarrel, but how, here on the stage, do we now produce a tent? Brutus proposes that he and Cassius

16 *Julius Caesar*, 4.2. 'Most noble brother, you have done me wrong.'

should go to his tent, and bids two of his people 'guard our door', and the two contingent 'armies' turn about and march off, back into the tiring-house. At this point in some modern editions a new scene (*Inside Brutus' tent*) is registered; but in the original there is no such thing. It says simply *Manet Brutus and Cassius* – they stay where they are, on stage. It has been suggested by earlier reconstructors of Elizabethan staging that the two generals might move back into the curtained 'discovery space' of the tiring-house, to give the literal effect of a tent, if only to begin with; but I think it may be seen from this (or any) drawing that that could never do. Neither is it needed. They simply stay where they are and have the whole stage for their great quarrel to range about on. There may be one or two stools to sit, kick, or put a foot on. Later a table is brought in with wine and cups, and later still a lighted taper for Brutus to read his book by. Then, with two of his officers lying asleep, and his taper burning low as he reads, Brutus is aware that the Ghost of Julius Caesar stands before him. How does this happen? Does the Ghost arise from a stage-trap hidden behind the table? Does it part the curtains and come forward from the back? Does it simply walk into view? I think this is no vengeful bloody spectre like Banquo's in *Macbeth*, but rather an evocation of the dignity of Brutus' conscience. It vanishes: but how? Perhaps again by the hidden trap. We know the methods by which the Elizabethans might have achieved such an effect, but their actual interpretation of them is another matter.

THE MERCHANT OF VENICE

The stage as I show it here set for this play (fig. 17a and b), though it is differently equipped than previously for *Julius Caesar*, has a certain special similarity which should now be noted. It may be seen in my pictures for *Romeo and Juliet* (figs. 12 and 13) that the scenic architectural details of the tiring-house frontage – pilasters, mouldings, etc. – are all structural, built in the round; whereas in *Caesar*, and here for *The Merchant of Venice*, the frontage of the tiring-house is a flat wall, only pierced for doors and windows, as it was shown by van Buchel for the Swan, and here also (fig. 11) for *Richard II*. But the 'architectural' detail for the tiring-house front in *Caesar* and *The Merchant* is all a painted decoration, executed in a lively 'folk-art' style, to give a grand effect rather than to deceive the eye with a supposed reality. We cannot know for certain how much of this was done. We do know that much of the Swan theatre was decorated with the old painter-decorators' trick of false marbling, and that the London theatres were, generally, all painted within. They are variously described by their contemporaries as 'painted theatres', 'gorgeous playing places' and 'sumptuous theatre houses'. I have supposed for reasons that will appear more obviously later, that the wall of the tiring-house facade itself was painted to resemble dressed stone, and I have here copied a treatment shown in sixteenth-century prints of the Italian Commedia dell'Arte for their portable canvas 'houses'. (There are similar examples from prints of pageant decorations erected in Jacobean London.)

I have in this instance tried to make do without a built-in 'discovery space' such as I have shown in *Romeo and Juliet*, and have instead erected a kind of tent or pavilion against the facade wall, within which to set up the row of caskets with their riddles for Portia's suitors. This will also serve, as may be seen, as the canopy of the Duke's chair of state in the Trial Scene in Act 4. Even so, in either case it would be necessary to have a door at the back within the curtains, to enable the setting-up of these properties to be quietly and discreetly done. Then, upon her entry with the Prince of Morocco, Portia bids her people: 'Go, draw the curtains and discover the several caskets to this noble Prince'.

The scenes with the caskets as I have shown them here require comment on two other points. First, the arrival of the Prince of Morocco in 2.7, and his meeting with Portia, must have been a formal entry from both of the main doors by two trains of grand people who meet at the centre. One might therefore suppose that they should take the processional way 'about' the stage as shown for Brutus and Cassius in fig. 16. But this is not a meeting in a public place out of doors: it is an interior scene, as in a hall, and I feel that to have the two groups converging across a smaller space towards the middle would give that feeling better. The second point concerns the placing of musicians. These are not specifically called for in the Morocco scene, but a musical accompaniment would be likely, certainly appropriate, and so I have placed them conventionally in the gallery on the upper part of the stage at the back. But in the next casket scene 3.2 (fig. 17b) with

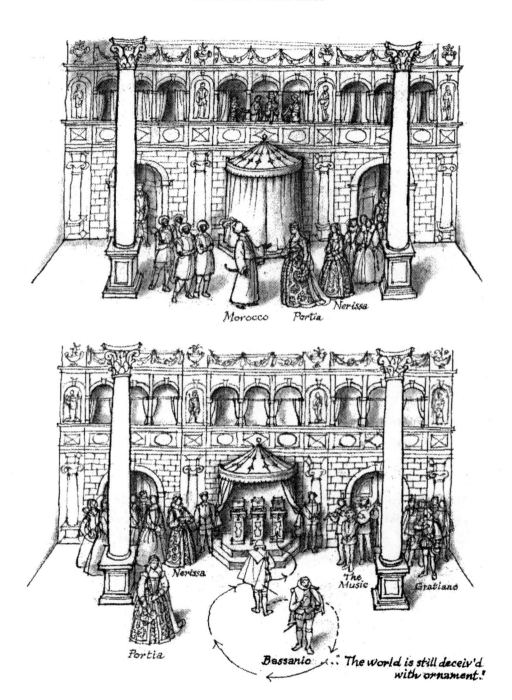

Morocco   Portia   Nerissa

Nerissa   The Music   Gratiano

Portia   Bassanio   ∴ The world is still deceiv'd
                                with ornament.'

17 *The Merchant of Venice*, (a) 2.7; (b) 3.2.

Bassanio pondering his choice of a casket, I have brought the musicians down onto the stage below, to be near him. The reason is that Shakespeare in this scene has emphasised the importance of the music by writing an encouraging, not to say hint-giving song for it (a succession of syllables rhyming with 'lead', the metal of the preferable casket). This is to be sung *whilst Bassanio comments on the caskets to himself*, and one feels that the boy singing should be seen and heard close to Bassanio who is standing, perhaps with his back to us, deep in thought. Then the song being over, Bassanio turns about, pronounces a moralising soliloquy and makes, to our relief, his proper choice.

A last observation for this section: it will be seen in the drawings for *Julius Caesar*, and in others throughout, that I have surrounded the stage on its three open sides with a low railing. This feature is referred to in some (but few) play texts, and appears in some (but few) mid-seventeenth-century drawings. Was it a usual thing, was it necessary or was it done at all in the public theatres? It does not appear in the Swan drawing. Yet I am inclined to like it, and have put it into many of my drawings, though, I must admit, rather inconsistently. Actors have suggested to me that it could have been a useful safety measure, to mark the distance, by a quick glance, to the edge of the stage: Elizabethan stages were built high, between five and six feet off the ground, a dangerous fall. It has also been suggested that the railing was there to prevent people in the audience from clambering onto the stage; but in fact it would rather assist than prevent this. I have imagined how an actor might have used the rail to lean upon with his foot, to address the audience (fig. 29); and there is a stage direction in one play in which two characters *sit on the rails*. I have also to acknowledge that for making illustrations of the stage the railing sometimes comes in very helpfully as a feature in pictorial composition, and so I am apt to favour it occasionally for my own illustrational purposes. The reader may be better advised by the authority of Professor Wickham: 'My own conclusion' he says, 'is that rails . . . were a prominent feature of some stages, especially in the later playhouses, but were not regarded as essential.'[4]

4 Glynne Wickham, *Early English Stages*, vol. 2, part 2, p. 178.

CHAPTER FOUR

THE SIEGE OF THE MUSIC ROOM

•

THE FIRST PART OF KING HENRY THE SIXTH; KING JOHN; THE TAMING OF THE SHREW

The last of the major public playhouses to be established in Shakespeare's London was the Red Bull. Like the first of them, the Theatre of 1576, it was located in a suburb to the north of London, at a safe distance beyond the restrictive jurisdiction of the Lord Mayor and the Common Council of the City. The old Theatre had been dismantled in 1598 and its timbers taken away to frame the polygonal round of the Globe, over on Bankside. The Red Bull was set up as a playhouse in or about 1605. It appears to have been a square theatre like the Fortune nearby, and like the others it had galleries and an open yard, unroofed. It had probably been converted out of an inn of the same name. We are concerned with it here because of its long life and popularity, evidently carrying with it into the very last years of the play-house tradition all the modes of stagecraft developed in the earlier time of Shakespeare and the Chamberlain's Men. Its most notable playwright was Thomas Heywood, whose four plays of the Golden, Silver, Brazen and Iron Ages presented at the Red Bull a grand spectacular panorama of ancient mythology from the birth of Jupiter to the fall of Troy, using all the resources of mechanical stagecraft then available on the public stage.[1] During all the reign of James I and of King Charles before the Civil War, while Ben Jonson was developing his comedies of social criticism, and he and the architect/designer Inigo Jones together were contriving elaborate entertainments for the Court Masques in Whitehall, the Red Bull, a mile

---

1 See G .F .Reynolds, *The Staging of Elizabethan Plays at the Red Bull Theatre* (New York, 1940.), *passim.*

away in the suburb of Clerkenwell, was maintaining a boisterous reputation as a popular playhouse of the old style.

Jonson died in 1638. There was no major poet then to write for him such a noble valedictory as he had done for his friend Shakespeare, but still there was a *Tribute to the Memory of Ben Jonson* written by an admiring younger poet, Jasper Mayne, who extols him as the great master of proper classical discipline in playwrighting, contrasting him – which is our concern here – with the old-style fustian stuff still to be witnessed at the Red Bull. I extract here the lines from his *Tribute* that are of immediate interest. Mayne addresses Jonson:

> Thy scene was free from Monsters, no hard plot
> Call'd down a God t'untie the unlikely knot.
> Thy stage was still a stage, two entrances
> Were not two parts o' the World disjoyn'd by Seas.
> Thine were land Tragedies, no Prince was found
> To swim a whole Scene out, then o' th' Stage drowned.
> Pitcht fields, as Red Bull wars, still felt thy doom,
> Thou laidst no sieges to the Music Room . . .

It seems that most cultivated persons at that later time scorned such stagy practices as the Red Bull provided. Jonson in his Prologue to *Every Man In His Humour* had specifically disowned the spectacle of an ancient god descending from Heaven in a 'creaking Throne', as an entertainment suitable only for 'the boys'. Mayne's 'two entrances' we have seen in the Swan picture, and, some ten years before that was drawn, Sir Philip Sidney had ridiculed the pretence that they should represent two different parts of the world: 'Asia of one side and Africa of the other, and so many other under kingdoms that the player, when he cometh in, must ever begin with telling where he is' . . . 'Now ye shall have three ladies walk to gather flowers, and then we must believe the stage to be a garden. . . . While in the meantime two armies fly in, represented with four swords and bucklers, and then what hard heart will not receive it for a pitched field?' This at once brings to mind Shakespeare's apology in *Henry V* for his 'four or five most vile and ragged foils' which he fears 'shall much disgrace the name of Agincourt'. Shakespeare in his time used all of those conventions, and in his hands the name of Agincourt was not disgraced by them. However, if Jasper Mayne had himself witnessed the old system still in action towards the end of the career of the Red Bull it must by then have been very shabby and out of breath – the last gasp of the tradition Shakespeare had inherited and for which he wrote without compunction during most of his life. Mayne's Prince who would 'swim a whole scene out' has more than an echo of Shakespeare's late Prince Pericles in it; and his 'pitcht fields, as Red Bull wars', though they may have felt Mayne's and Ben Jonson's 'doom', were given full rein in Shakespeare's earlier days at the Rose and the Theatre, with his three plays of *Henry the Sixth*; and as to laying 'sieges to the Music Room', Shakespeare had laid a memorable one, in the first of the three, which took place over four scenes, with a total of more than two hundred lines.

THE FIRST PART OF KING HENRY VI

The siege in question, is the siege of Orleans by the English in 1429. The stage has now to represent the besieged city and its walls. The action begins simply with the entry of two figures, a man and a boy. The man tells us that he is the Chief Master Gunner of Orleans, and describes to the boy, his apprentice, how he has set a loaded gun aimed at 'yonder tower' where, he has learned, the English commanders will come 'to a secret grate of iron bars' to spy into the town and make their plans against it. The Gunner then says he has to leave his post for some other duty for a while, but before going he tells the boy to keep watch, and to fetch him when the English appear. Then they both exit separately, with the boy, as he goes, declaring to the audience his intention to fire the gun himself without troubling his master the Gunner. What now follows is a complex of activity which I have brought together into the two pictures in fig. 8, numbering the different incidents in sequence. First the English commanders, the Earl of Salisbury and Lord Talbot with at least two others, now enter, as the stage direction says *on the turrets* which I assume at this point must be the main part of the upper-stage. After some thirty-seven lines of dialogue 'on this turret's top' they then seem to have moved and posted themselves at a window, as I have shown them in the drawing (1), for Salisbury is saying 'here through this grate. . . .

I view the Frenchmen how they fortify' (though it is also possible the 'grate' was merely 'supposed', and presented from the upper-stage in mime). But shortly before this we have the direction: *'Enter the boy with a linstock'* (2). The Gunner's boy we must at once recognise, and it is likely he will in the first place have been given some distinctive aid to quick recognition, such as, for example, a red bonnet. His linstock is a staff which holds the match that is to fire the gun. So now we have the English on their tower, and the boy with the burning match, and the scene is set for the shooting; but where is the gun? It is sometimes suggested that this has already been positioned on the stage, or even perhaps placed in some part of the galleries overlooking it, aiming towards the stage-house; or else that a dummy gun, or mimic action, would have been used for this scene, with a noise of gunfire made by a bang on a drum. I think none of that very likely. Something more sensational has to happen here. The stage direction says: *Here they shot, and Salisbury falls down.* (3)

Elizabethan theatrical gunfire was always used for a grand effect. It was an eagerly expected excitement, with the real noise and smell of real gunfire and powder. A mere imitation made by drums would never do, nor some half-charge pop from a dummy cannon. But neither would it have been practical, let alone safe, to discharge a real gun, even though only blank-loaded with wadding, within the circle of a crowded theatre. So here the noise of cannon-fire was real, and was probably discharged on open ground at the back of the tiring-house. (It was from there, in 1613, that a burning wad from such a discharge was carried upwards on a current of air into the thatched roof of the Globe. It burned the building down.) The noise outside would be heard to good effect inside the theatre because of its unroofed yard – it was a special effect belonging to the open-yarded public theatres alone. In this play of *Henry VI* it was used not only here at the shooting of Salisbury, but in a later scene where a French countess seeks to entrap Lord Talbot in her castle; but at a critical moment he gives a signal, and there is heard at once a great salvo of gunfire – in the stage direction: *a peal of ordinance* – while his soldiers enter the stage on all sides.

The gunfire effect in theatres was not caused by a gun, but by a component part of one, the firing-chamber, which in certain types of ordnance

18 *The First Part of King Henry VI*, 1.4. A frame for operating
offstage gunfire with 'chambers' (conjectural).

could be lifted out separately with a handle, for charging and re-loading. Thus in stage directions these pieces are called 'chambers'. An illustration imagining how they might have been set up is given in fig. 18. It can hardly be doubted that the 'gun' which was to shoot down the Earl of Salisbury was of this kind. If so, we may imagine the whole scene as follows: while the English commanders are busy with their plans on the 'turrets', the Gunner's boy enters the stage below with his smoking match and linstock (2). He creeps round and spies the English at their window. He then blows on his match, or perhaps even swings it around, to make it glow brightly; and then either with significant 'gunfire gestures' for the benefit of the audience, he runs off stage with it; or, perhaps better, he might there on the stage mimic the action of firing the gun. In either event, on the instant we hear the noise of the gun, (but *outside* the theatre), and *Salisbury falls down* (3).

We now have a problem of visibility by which the height of the upper-stage may be judged. Salisbury and one other knight, Sir Thomas Gargrave, lie dying on the upper-stage floor. Lord Talbot and several soldiers (there have to be at least enough of them to carry off bodies later) are unhurt. There is now a scene of some forty lines wherein Talbot addresses the two dying men in such a way as to help dramatise their agonies for the audience. Then there enters a messenger with the news that 'Joan La Pucelle . . . is come with great power to raise the seige', and at this *Here Salisbury lifteth himself up and groans*. What now has to be understood is that this upper-stage must be not only spacious enough for all this action to take place, but that the dying Salisbury writhing on the floor, and later lifting himself up and groaning, must all be clearly seen by the audience, including the crowded 'groundlings' standing some way below in the yard. It follows therefore that, for this play at least, there cannot be any parapet or balustrade along the front of the upper-stage, preventing a view of the fallen men. So now a further calculation has to be made: the height of the upper-stage above the lower. It will be understood that for some of the understanding audience in the yard below, their view of the upper-stage would be like looking towards a high shelf, above eye level, so that an actor lying on the floor of it would need to be well towards the front if he were not to disappear as it were below its 'horizon'. (Normally of course, with actors simply seated or standing on the upper-stage this difficulty does not arise). Meanwhile there are certain factors which may help to establish a height for the upper-stage floor above the lower. First, it must be high enough to allow a fairly generous head-height for the doorways beneath it; but having allowed for that the height above it may be fairly estimated from events that happen in a further on in the scene. Salisbury is dead and Joan La Pucelle, at whose name he had so prophetically groaned, has driven off the English and relieved the town. The English will recapture it, however; and so we turn to the lower sketch in the illustration on p. 22.

We are still at the city of Orleans, at the beginning of Act 2, which has opened with the entry of a French serjeant and two sentinels, evidently upon the upper-stage 'walls' of the town. The serjeant sets the sentinels to their posts and leaves them, and when he has gone the others settle down grumblingly to sleep, or so it must seem, for they do not observe what happens next: *Enter Talbot, Bedford and Burgundy, with scaling ladders: their drums beating a dead march.* The English lords and Burgundy set up their ladders to the walls in three different places: ('I'll to yond corner,' . . . 'And I'll to this' . . . 'And here will Talbot mount'). They all ascend the walls, and the sentinels, too late, give the alarm, while the allies with their cries of 'St George!' and 'A Talbot!' go in, above, driving out the French, for immediately after that comes the stage direction: *The French leap o'er the walls in their shirts* (4). Then: *Enter several ways* . . . (i.e. by different doors presumably on the stage below) the escaping French nobles *half ready and half unready* (5), and they are joined by Charles the Dauphin and Joan La Pucelle (6). Later *'they fly, leaving their clothes behind'*, which an English soldier collects for 'spoils'. In a later act, at another siege at Rouen, Joan makes a signal for an attack on the town by entering *on the top, thrusting out a torch burning.* The signal is also described in the dialogue as being given 'from, yonder tower'. I have tried to locate a suitable 'top' for her on the battlemented tower at (7), but the term is obscure. Shakespeare uses it only in one other place, in 3.3 of *The Tempest*, where Prospero is watching a scene on the stage below. The stage direction there begins: *Solemn and strange Musicke: and Prosper on the top (invisible).* In this case it would be reasonable to see 'the top' as being the top of the projecting 'porch' which I have conjectured frequently among my drawings herein, as for *The Tempest* (fig. 46, p. 134). But that is a digression from which we should return now to the siege of Orleans, which may help us to solve a problem.

The problem is two-fold: what was the height of the 'walls' to the upper-stage, and what was the actual length of the scaling-ladder the actors had to climb to enter the town? It may be remembered that Malone's guess was that the floor of this upper-stage at the back (which he called a 'balcony') was 'eight or nine feet' above the lower floor. In my general diagram p. 25 I have set it at 9 feet 6 inches, and I am coming to think that may be rather too high. Let me here reduce it to nine feet only. For a wall that high, a ladder set against it at a reasonable climbing angle of 15° would have to be 9 feet 4 inches long, without allowing any spare length over the top to help the climber get off easily onto the upper level. To store three ladders of that length in the tiring-house would be possible, and to get them out of a door seven feet high by five feet wide would be possible also, but to do it neatly and set them up featly in performance would possibly require two men to handle each ladder, not counting the three lords who have to mount them, nor the *Drummers beating a Dead March* (stated as plural, so there must be at least two); so we now have eleven actors, three long ladders and two drums; no great matter, perhaps, but nevertheless quite a business to prepare in the tiring-house. But with all this we are provided with some practical dimensions for establishing that the height of the upper-stage at the siege of Orleans, allowing headroom for the movement of actors and their paraphernalia underneath, must have been about nine feet, not much more, nor less. We may now test the effect of this with a scene from another play of about the same date (the early 1590s).

KING JOHN

The scene is 4.3. The young Prince Arthur, the proper claimant to the English throne, has been captured by King John and entrusted to his minister Hubert De Burgh with the cruel instruction to blind him and kill him. The long scene in which the pathetic pleading of the boy prevails upon the underlying goodness of Hubert's real nature, to spare him, was in earlier times (and may at any time become again) one of the great 'dramatic acting

19 *King John*, 4.3. Arthur: 'The wall is high, and yet will I leap down.'

pieces' in the Shakespeare canon. So the prince is left alone and alive in prison, and determines to escape. Our scene now opens with the direction: *Enter Arthur on the walles* (fig. 19). Here we see the walls of the English prison very much as we left them at French Orleans, but I have here put them into a different theatre with an arrangement for the upper-stage similar to that in my original diagram (fig. 10). As shown there, the upper-stage is not opened out, but is closed all along its front by an arcade of windows, such as at the Swan, although as in the diagram, there is an opening at the centre allowing the boy actor playing Prince Arthur to come through onto the top of the projecting doorway piece. The height of this upper-stage floor I have supposed, as at Orleans, to be nine feet. To stand at an upper window at that height and look down to the ground is to decide at once that it is no height for making a standing jump without some thought. And here stands young Arthur preparing to do so. 'The wall is high' he says, and he has a speech of eight lines before he leaps to his death.

It will be seen in my drawing that I have thoughtfully provided a cushion of rushes for the young actor to land on – they are from the rushes normally provided for strewing over the stage. That would have helped soften his landing, but even more helpfully the boy will have needed to be specially trained, not only for the dramatic gesture of the drop itself but for his safety in landing, without injury. True, the boy was only *acting* his fall, and its great height was mostly a pretence, but even so, a nine-foot drop is enough to knock the breath out of you unless you are specially prepared for it, and the fallen boy has still two lines of a dying speech to make as he expires. But a probability that the young actor was in fact specially prepared for his leap is supported by two things. First, we know that there existed in the London theatre at the time an athletic group known as 'John Symonds and Mr Standley's Boys', who were noted for 'tumbling' and for 'feats of activity and vaulting'; there was, therefore, an established tradition for the training of such young performers. The second thing is that before Arthur enters *on the walles* for his final scene, he had changed his clothes. We have seen him throughout the play dressed as a young prince, in courtly clothes, neatly trussed and buttoned at all points. He was presumably dressed like this even when we last saw him, pleading with Hubert for mercy. One would suppose that when we next see him, alone, attempting to escape, he must be instantly recognisable as soon as he appears. But he is not. We have never before seen him dressed as he now is, and he has quickly to explain the reason why this is. In order to escape unrecognised among the people in the town, he says, he has had to disguise himself in 'this ship-boy's semblance'. A ship-boy's working clothes were loose and easy, with baggy pantaloons, suitable for climbing and hauling and working on deck. The young actor here had not only been athletically trained for an effective leap, but had also changed into a 'jump-suit' for the purpose. However, the 'ship-boy's semblance' does not for a moment deceive the lords who, in the lower picture, discover the body of the young Prince, and vow the consequent downfall of the wicked king.

Meanwhile if it may be agreed that nine feet is a suitable height for an upper-stage 'castle' or fortified town, both for leaping down from and assaulting with scaling ladders, it may also be useful at this point to consider the development of this aspect of the Elizabethan playhouse stage at the end of the sixteenth century. The stage-house as a fortress under siege was popular not only as a spectacle in its own right, as we have seen in this play of Henry VI, but from earlier medieval times as a moral metaphor of the human condition. The most famous example in English is the play of *The Castle of Perseverance* dating from 1425, wherein Mankind defends his fortress 'tower', set in the midst of a circular auditorium forty-five feet in diameter, against all the assaults of the Devil and the Deadly Sins.[2] Also, in Anthony Munday's *John a Kent and John a Cumber*, a play which belonged to the Admiral's Men at the Rose and was performed there probably in the early 1590s, the stage-house is repeatedly referred to in stage-directions as *The Castell*, into which the actors enter and appear again 'on the walls'. From such evidences over a span of different plays I have thought it worthwhile to try to imagine the development of a theatre stage-house from an early castle-like style into the more familiar facade, with its overhead Heavens and supporting posts, which we know from the Swan. A group of numbered sketches illustrating such a development is given opposite.

2 See *The Medieval Theatre in the Round* by Richard Southern (London, Faber and Faber, 1957).

Experiments for an
Elizabethan staging
for the Henry VI &
Richard III plays.
(here shown with &
without the addition
of a "Heavens"
Superstructure)
CWH 1985

20 Development of the tiring-house frontage as a castle or city wall,
with the later addition of The Heavens superstructure.

Sketch 1 is a 'castle' house centred at the back of the stage within the enclosing timber-framed polygon of the playhouse, with the two entry doors to the stage, one on each side of it. This might have been an early adaptation of the Theatre of 1576, still in touch with a medieval tradition. Sketch 2 is developed from the foregoing, to increase the space in the tiring-house by building its frontage forward on a straight line enclosing three (or more) bays of the polygon. A floor over the new, enlarged part of the tiring-house now forms an upper-stage, which is extended further by the 'porch' section of the old 'castle'. In picture 3 the walls and castle gate have been taken and put back in line with the tiring-house, leaving a sort of porch which can be hung with curtains and used if needed as a closed-off 'discovery space'. All of this is imagined as an early development, before 1592, the year when Henslowe installed his stage roof and posts at the Rose. Picture 4 now shows the effect with the roof and posts added, and the 'porch' removed. There remains the open space of the upper-stage between two windowed 'houses', and the upper-stage might now at any time be provided with a railing or balustrade across the front. With this arrangement, since many plays, perhaps a majority, for most of the time had no need for an extensive upper-stage, the space could be used as a private room for privileged audiences, say, for a noble patron and his friends. Thus we arrive at a lords' room 'over the stage' or 'over the tyerhowsse' which appears as an expense in Henslowe's accounts in 1592. This upper space also appears as a parody of itself in both its uses, for both lords and actors, in the Induction to Shakespeare's *The Taming of the Shrew*, as we shall see. Before that, however, we must take note of the last development (5) in my series of sketches. Here the upper-stage, as such, has gone. Its space has been filled across by a panelled balustrade and a range of windows, perhaps even divided into separate rooms or boxes, giving something of the effect we see in the drawing of the Swan, although here I have retained a central doorway or curtained opening. I have retained also a vestige of the old castle with which it all began, by a painted frieze of 'battlements' along the top.

I ought to emphasise, before leaving this group of sketches, that although they are laid out as a sequence they are not intended to offer themselves as a theory for the sequential development, step by step like this, of some 'typical' Shakespearean playhouse. Such a wide-ranging piece of guesswork could not possibly be all true and correct in itself. But perhaps with caution it could be seen as set of variations upon a theme of the general style and character of the public playhouse stages, details from which could have been shared among different theatres. To me it suggests itself as having a common grandparent in the style of a medieval castle – possibly much simpler than the one I have drawn – and in at least one theatre there must have been an upper-stage suitable for the sieges and scaling ladders of Shakespeare's *Henry VI*.[3] But Jasper Mayne at the latter end of the public playhouse time, said ironically that theatre sieges were laid not to castles but 'to the music room'. Presumably by that time it had become more or less the same thing. We may here consider a step in that transition.

THE TAMING OF THE SHREW

The only recorded date and theatre for this popular play during Shakespeare's lifetime, was when Henslowe staged it in his theatre at Newington Butts, in the summer of 1594. Before that date, for nearly two years there had been a severe outbreak of plague in London: all the theatres had been closed by law for fear of contagion, the player companies had been obliged to take to the road in the provinces, and Henslowe had taken advantage of the enforced closure to enlarge and alter his Rose on Bankside. Newington Butts was three-quarters of a mile south of Bankside, just beyond the authority of the City Council. Henslowe's theatre there was evidently small and old-fashioned, but when he re-opened it with the ending of the plague both the Admiral's and the Chamberlain's companies and Shakespeare, went to work in it, before moving back again to Bankside. In my drawings for Professor Thompson's edition of *The Taming of the Shrew* which are reproduced here I attempted to reconstruct the Newington Butts theatre as a small playhouse in the style as conventionally imagined when I made these drawings, some years before the remains of the Rose theatre

---

3 There are other sieges by other authors, requiring the same facilities, of about the same period. Cf. the anonymous *Allarum for London or The Siege of Antwerp c.* 1600; and Thomas Lodge's *The Wounds of Civil War: The True Tragedies of Marius and Scilla c.* 1588. And there are others. The presentation of sieges and castle walls was at this time very popular.

were excavated in 1989, with its evidence that the earlier playhouses may not all have had post-supported roofs over their stages. My reconstruction, therefore, was still based upon the Swan in that respect, though I had seen fit to enlarge the upper-stage or 'lords' room' area, because of what now follows in *The Shrew*.

Our concern here is with the two preliminary scenes of the play which are known as the Induction. In the first of these scenes the drunken tinker Christopher Sly, being thrust out of an alehouse to sleep off his booziness on the ground, is found there by a noble lord and his hunting party. The lord conceives it as an entertaining example to 'practise' on this boor, to have him wake into sweet gentleness and luxury, and observe the effect of these graces upon his grossness; and so he bids his huntsmen pick up Sly and carry him off to his mansion. At this moment a company of travelling players happens to arrive, whom the lord at once includes in his 'practise', engaging one of their boy players to dress in his stage woman's gear and present himself as Sly's long forgotten 'wife'. All this takes place upon the main stage, below. It is the next scene, known as Induction 2, which now provides our subject.

The original text, as printed in the Shakespeare First Folio, directs that the whole of Induction 2 is to be played 'aloft', that is, on the upper-stage. It is a scene lasting about fifteen minutes, involving some nine or ten actors of whom at least six are present on that upper-stage the whole time, with others coming and going. Also involved are a group of musicians and a messenger, though these need not and I think did not then appear on the upper-stage. The scene, curiously, may be understood in two different ways, both together and at once. First it holds together the story-line of the drunkard and his awakening as into a dream; while at the same time it is all nothing but a play in a playhouse. What the audience are looking at is the 'lord's room' over the stage, where they see the player lord himself acting the part of his own steward, managing his own servants in the deception of the awakening mock-lord. The inverted comedy becomes farcical when the red-nosed Sly is confronted with his 'wife', though there is then a sudden moment of pathos with his 'I would be loath to fall into my dreams again'. Then the messenger enters on (as I think) the stage below, to announce that the players are ready with their comedy, while on the upper-stage the lord-as-steward

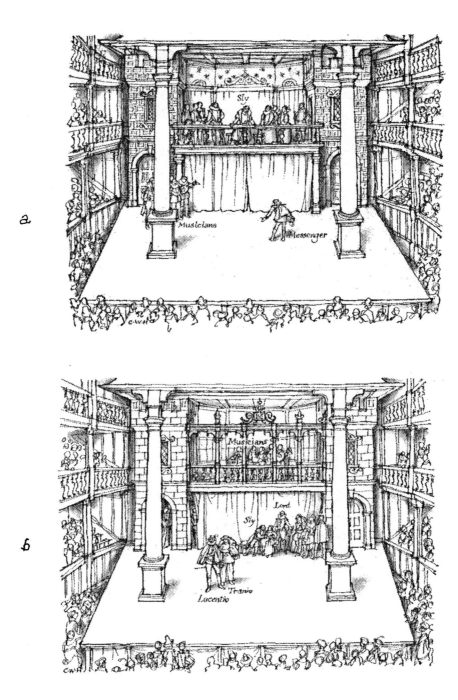

21 *The Taming of the Shrew.* Alternative stagings for the Induction: (a) with the Christopher Sly scenes placed 'above' and (b) on the main stage.

directs the placing of chairs and stools for the mock-lord Sly and his 'Lady' at the front rail overlooking the stage, with a table of drink and dainties, and attendants, all as the playhouse audience has seen it often before when lords and gentlemen have taken their private rooms above or beside the stage. So in this case the lords' room over the stage has become a travesty of itself.

That having been said, it should now be said also that it is possible to doubt whether all the Induction scene was in fact played *aloft* as the stage-direction implies it was. Professor Thompson, for whose edition of the play[4] my illustration (fig. 21a) was originally made, argues very carefully that for such an extended scene the situation was really neither practical nor typical of the gallery's use, and suspects that the word *aloft* in the relevant stage-direction was put in or left in by mistake. If that were true, the only alternative presentation of the scene would have to be below, on the main stage. This would not only meet all Professor Thompson's objections but has other advantages of its own: for one thing, it is certain that a company taking this play on tour would not expect to find such a convenient gallery space over a temporary stage as I have drawn here, to give the effect I describe; so they would normally think of their staging as all on one level. Therefore, though I personally stand by my upper-stage interpretation and do not think the *aloft* in the text is any mistake, I was happy not to dispute the alternative solution, but to make the alternative drawing of it which I show at (fig. 21b). One advantage of this arrangement is that as the proper or main play of *The Shrew* takes over the action on the stage, the characters of the Induction can discreetly remove themselves, and their departure, even in the end their total absence, will not be noticed.

There remains one further thing of interest here: the Induction calls for music, and therefore musicians: ('Wilt thou have music? Hark, Apollo plays / And twenty caged nightingales do sing'). With the first arrangement, having all the Induction played 'aloft', there could be no room aloft for the musicians, as well as for so many actors, and so I have stationed them

---

4 *The Taming of the Shrew*, ed. Ann Thompson (Cambridge Unversity Press, *New Cambridge Shakespeare*, 1984).

below, on the main stage. With the second arrangement, however, the action being all on the lower stage, the gallery above is readily available for the musicians, who occupy it as they do by custom in the great hall galleries of colleges and noble houses. In effect, the upper-stage, has now become the Music Room.

CHAPTER FIVE

ENTER THE WHOLE ARMY

•

ALL'S WELL THAT ENDS WELL; THE THIRD PART OF KING HENRY VI; ANTONY AND CLEOPATRA (1)

ALL'S WELL THAT ENDS WELL

This play has a certain identity of its own, like an odd link attached out of context to one side of the chain of Shakespeare's earlier masterpieces. Its composition is generally placed by scholars somewhere between 1597 and 1602, that is at the time of *Romeo and Juliet*, the *Henry IV* plays, *Henry V* and *The Merchant of Venice*, the first flush of the dramatist's high tide. From internal evidence it seems certain it was in fact put on the stage, but there is no record to tell us when. It was included in the canon of the First Folio with the authority of the author's personal friends and colleagues, but its text is peppered with editorial oversights and printers' errors. Yet in spite of, perhaps even because of, that it has for us here a particular interest. It appears to have been put together either from Shakespeare's draft papers or from the stage book-holder's working copy, straight out of the tiring-house, or perhaps from both of these together, which the printer then collated and set up in type just as it stood. For example some of the stage-directions seem to be more like the author's preliminary notes than a standing instruction for actors: *Enter the king with divers young lords, taking leave for the Florentine war* . . . the 'young lords' and the leave-taking are then immediately duplicated in the spoken dialogue. Or: *Parolles and Lafeu stay behind, commenting of this wedding*, which at once they do at length, without the slightest need of a stage-direction. In other places the names of characters in the play, indicating the lines they are to speak, are suddenly replaced by the initials of the actors who are to speak them, a substitution evidently made in the book-holder's working copy. Thus by accident the tiring-house and its problems, the preparation of the actors and all their gear, is brought to our attention. We have to imagine the busy crowded backstage with everyone bustling on tip-toe and talking in whispers as they listen for the cue-lines on the stage out there, and prepare for their entry. And with this I come to a stage-direction in 3.5 which is the cue for this chapter: *Drum and Colours Enter Count Rossillion, Parolles, and the whole army*

The whole army? As a stage-direction it is unusual and suggestive: but what exactly does it suggest, and who wrote the words into the script? It seems from its context more likely to have been written in by the book-holder, as a memorandum to alert the tiring-house staff, who would have to organise what was clearly intended to be a spectacular parade around the stage – a victorious army returning from the wars – rather than a simple stage-direction by the author. The author has created his dramatic idea, assuming from experience that it could be done, but it was the book-holder and the stage-keeper who would have to summon up the resources for doing it. So how many people had the company at its disposal at that time, and how much room was there in that crowded tiring-house to get an 'army' ready for the stage?

Space backstage must have been limited at the best of times. The hugger-mugger shown in my drawing on p. 73 is perhaps too romantic, and much of the picturesque gear I have dispersed about the place could have been more safely stored out of the way. Henslowe, probably, kept most of his large collection of properties and costumes above in the attic storey. The back-stage space at the Globe at stage-level may be imagined as a curved strip about sixty-five feet long but only twelve feet deep, interrupted by wooden posts and stairways, and with whatever furniture would be needed for the stage in the next scenes – beds or thrones or whatever might be – standing in the way. Possibly for dressing-rooms and other services, the companies at the established theatres may have had the use of a shed or of some other buildings nearby. Hollar's late etching of the Globe shows a convenient house at the back which I assume could have been taken over for such purposes; and even the very first playhouse, the Theatre of 1576, had a

Drum and Colours

Antonio

Escalus

Bertram

Parolles

"Lose our drum! Well...."

Widow

Diana

Helena

Violenta

Mariana

C.W.H.

22 *All's Well That Ends Well, 3.5. Drum and Colours . . . Enter . . . the whole army.*

23 A view in the tiring-house. Note the bookholder's desk and the 'platt'
(brief running order) of the play on the wall.

tumbledown barn behind it, which was conveniently buttressed up against the Theatre (for its own stability) and might have provided valuable extra space.[1] It can be seen on the left of figure 1.

Of the player companies themselves, the successful ones with their permanent theatres in London were larger organisations than is generally supposed. Romance remembers them in their earlier times as strolling players, a picturesque few with their cartful of props and costumes, tramping from town to town. They might of course have reverted to that condition at any time, as Edward Alleyn did during the great plague of 1592–4 when the London theatres were closed (and Philip Henslowe used the occasion to rebuild and enlarge his Rose theatre), but in the settled permanency of the London playhouses it had become a very different matter, as Professor Baldwin has shown.[2] The actors, having established themselves as a profession, were quick to consolidate and protect it as a recognised craft. They took on boy actors for training, and they engaged the services of hired men in every department.

The corporate and controlling membership of the actors' companies themselves was strictly – and jealously – limited. The Chamberlain's Men had an established membership of only eight, of whom, after 1594, Shakespeare was one. (In the next reign, when they became the King's Men, the membership was increased by three.) Full membership could be attained from among the hired actors of the general company, or by boy actors or young men who had served their time in training, but only when there was a vacancy by death or retirement. But beyond this elite membership the attached body of hired men was very numerous. There were aspiring freelance actors, musicians, backstage management staff including 'tire-men' and 'tire-women', carpenters and painters, and 'gatherers' to take the money at the entrances to the different parts of the theatre. Baldwin estimates there could hardly have been less than twenty of these at each playhouse. They might also have served as cleaners and general handymen. And

---

1 See Herbert Berry, *Shakespeare's Playhouses*, (New York, AMS Press, 1987).
2 T. W .Baldwin, *The Organization and Personnel of the Shakespearean Company*, (Princeton University Press, 1927).

then, besides all these, there were the apprentices. These would fall into two classes. A normal apprenticeship in accordance with the governing Statute of Artificers would be for seven years, and thus a youth apprenticed for the craft of acting would enter at sixteen – that is, after his voice had broken – and so finish his training as a young man of twenty-four, with hopes of becoming a full member of the company later on. These youths were apprenticed directly to individual actors who were their masters and trainers. But, besides these, the company also had special need of younger boys, such as formed the companies of boy players at the great choir-schools, of St Paul's and the Chapel Royal. These, in the public theatres, would provide the singers for Shakespeare's songs, or the choir of 'caged nightingales' that are offered to Christopher Sly at his awakening in the lord's bedchamber in *The Taming of the Shrew*.

These younger boys and the apprentices together, until they became fully-qualified actors, out of their time and presumably awaiting vacancies to become full members of the company, might together make up a school of some twenty or more young people, all available for the stage at any time during their training. So with this we may now revise that earlier calculation, based on the limitations of small travelling companies on the road. The establishment of the Chamberlain's Men when in occupation at the Globe could have numbered at least sixty persons, if not more. The fact that a whole repertory of elaborate plays could be learned and staged, usually for very short runs, and replaced and revived again at short notice, mixed in with jigs and tumbling and any other sort of up-to-the-moment entertainment, is very surprising; but it may be better understood if we allow that such a large establishment could well assemble two or three separate acting groups, to rehearse and take over from each other in quick succession. One such group could have been largely composed of apprentices, working together as a training company. The play of *All's Well That Ends Well* in many ways suggests this, and may indeed have been written with such a company in mind. It has a cast of seventeen characters, only six of whom stand out as being necessarily for older or more experienced actors: the rest could all be provided from the apprentice company. The leading character Bertram of Rossillion is himself described as young, and is accompanied to

75

the Florentine war by the 'young lords' noted above, and there is a much longer cast than usual of women's parts, the speciality for which all boy players were initially recruited and trained. Scholars are generally agreed that *All's Well That Ends Well* may be the same as a supposedly 'lost' play of Shakespeare's, *Love's Labour's Won*, a presumed successor to *Love's Labour's Lost*. It is at least worth noting here that the latter has all the same characteristics as *All's Well*: a cast of possibly youthful actors outnumbering the most likely older players by two to one, with a larger than usual proportion of woman's parts. There is also the similarity of both plays being set with the background of a romantic French courtly life, a setting unlike anything elsewhere in Shakespeare's work. Scholars appear divided about the dating of *All's Well*, (ranging widely between 1588 and 1602) but there seems to be a case for supposing it may be paired with *Love's Labour's Lost*, and was composed at around the same time for a similar group of actors. However, in a textual matter of this kind, which is not my proper field, it is perhaps temerarious of me to say so.

We may now return to that entry of the 'whole army', and its composition. The illustration on p. 72 shows the parade passing by as it were for inspection, and we may ask if this is what the resources of the company could have produced, and whether this is indeed the effect intended by that stage-direction. The drawing contains thirty-two characters, including the five 'women' spectators; so we have a 'whole army' of twenty-seven men, and presumably, from the resources of personnel we have been discussing, that number could indeed have been found and equipped. By timing the space of dialogue in which the spectators comment on the parade as it goes by, the whole thing could easily have been over in three or four minutes, yet in that short time it must have made an effective show. It is in fact the only 'spectacular' scene in the play and was not to be wasted. Let us agree that my picture shows the effect they would have *hoped* to make on their audience, but with all the movement, and with the noise of the drums, it might perhaps have been achieved with less people.

For the purposes of this illustration it has been useful to show the group of women spectators from the back, looking in, whereas on the stage in performance I imagine they would have been placed centre-stage between the two great posts, looking out towards the audience. The army would then pass by on the circuit 'about the stage', between them and the audience. The spectators' commentary would fill the gaps in the procession, and the movement, especially of the flags, would fill the stage. Flags in a modern procession are usually carried as an accent of high dignity, not moved nor flourished. In the theatre, in the confines of a modern proscenium stage, there is little choice but to carry them so, but this was neither the case nor the tradition on the wide, open stage of Shakespeare's theatre. It is safe to argue that flags were there brought in with a flourish as I show in my drawing. There is evidence for this, as many thousands of visitors to a famous and ancient pageant, the Palio horse race in Siena, can testify. That event is preceded by a long parade of all the competitive civic societies, the *contrade*, which own the horses, and each *contrada* has its own drum and colours. These flags are not only flourished about but thrown high into the air and caught again in a variety of long-practised exercises, while the drummers beat a ceremonious tattoo. The Palio is indeed a historical relic, but it is *not* a revival; it has survived more or less in its present form by direct continuity from the early seventeenth century, at which time the drum-and-colour ceremonial was widely practised and can be found as far afield as north-western Europe. This may be seen in a pair of popular engravings by the Dutch artist Hendrick Goltzius, who was contemporary with Shakespeare (figs. 24 and 25). The pictures date from 1587 and show a processional flag-bearer and drummer of that time. The size of the flag is a little hard to believe, and perhaps Goltzius, for the sake of his composition, may have exaggerated, but he makes it clear that the flag itself must have been of a light material, probably silk; and it should be noted that it has a very short length of staff below the spread, thus allowing it to be held up and flourished with one hand only. (The flag-bearer's 'peascod-bellied' doublet is not a exaggeration, but an item of high fashion at the time.)

The decoration and/or heraldry of these flags is a difficult subject. A silken flag divided into simple areas of colour could be made by stitching shaped pieces together, and more elaborate figures might be made by painting the silk with coloured dyes, but the use of more solid pigments would require a heavier fabric and might limit the flourishing effect. I will return to

24 and 25 Drummer and Standard-bearer. Etchings by H. Goltzius, 1587.

this in connection with *King Henry VI*, below. Meanwhile there are still some points to be taken up about the picture of the whole army on p. 72. In it there are two characters, Antonio and Escalus, who appear to make up the numbers of the army and are named as they pass by the women spectators, but who do not otherwise appear in any version of the play as we have it. Evidently they are noblemen and so I have given each of them a drum and a drummer, which adds to the general military excitement and noise. It may also help to emphasise the fact that the heroic young Count Bertram has no drum at all. It was captured by the enemy in the battle, and the cowardly braggart Parolles is here making a great 'melancholy' about the dishonour of it all, which will later lead to the comedy of his unmasking, in a further scene.

THE THIRD PART OF KING HENRY VI

It has here been supposed that the special mention of 'the Whole Army' implies something more elaborate in itself than the simpler convention of a leader with his flag and drum and perhaps one or two other soldiers, to represent a powerful force. This latter method is exemplified by Shakespeare in *The Third Part of King Henry VI*, where at the beginning of Act 5 we find the Earl of Warwick holding the town of Coventry for the Lancastrian cause, and awaiting the arrival of his allies. The town, as I show it in p. 80 is represented on the stage by the scenic device of the city gate and its battlements, placed centrally against the frontage of the upper stage. Warwick and the Mayor of Coventry and others are described as being 'upon the Walles'. The noise of a marching drum is heard at a distance off-stage, within the tiring-house, and we must suppose that this background noise is heard more or less continually during this scene which is concerned throughout with the arrival and alignment or re-alignment of armed forces on the sides of Lancaster and York. The Lancastrian Warwick hears the marching drum, but it is the Yorkist army that now enters (*March. Flourish. Enter Edward, Richard and Soldiers*), and send their trumpet 'to the Walles, to sound a Parle'. The parley itself, defiant and venomous with accusations of treachery, is accompanied with more drumming offstage as Warwick's Lancastrian allies arrive now in quick succession, the Earls of Oxford and

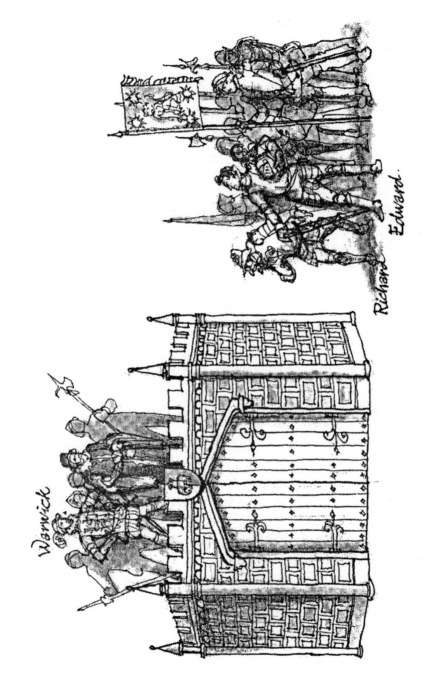

Warwick

Richard. *Edward.*

26 *The Third Part of King Henry VI*, 5.1. *Enter Warwick . . . and others upon the walls . . . Flourish. Enter Edward, Richard and soldiers.*

Somerset and the Marquess of Montague, each contingent with its *Drumme and Colours*. I have tried to create the cumulative effect of these arrivals in my drawing on p. 80. The reinforcing armies do in fact enter separately, and the gates of the town are opened to let them in, but the intervals between each arrival are short and the continuing noise of the drumming and the flamboyant flourishing of the colours and the exchanges of defiance between the two sides would I suggest be enough to fill the stage with action. Then the last contingent arrives, the Duke of Clarence with his *Drumme and his Colours*, but he does not enter the town, as expected, because he has now changed sides: he halts and lines up his 'army' outside, with the Yorkists. The scene finishes with a challenge to battle: the Yorkist army with the Duke of Clarence's force march from the stage; the town gates open again and Warwick and his company follow, with Oxford, Somerset and Montague and all their drums and colours, to martial music. The battle of Barnet is then immediately joined, mostly but one may suppose not entirely offstage, as suggested by the noisy cut and thrust of the stage-direction *Alarum, Retreat, Excursions, Exeunt*.

I have described that scene at some length because in doing so it brings us to a practical problem which, though it may not here be solved ought at least to be addressed: those so-called *Colours*. What in this context does the word mean? They were of course flags or banners and I have suggested that they were paraded upon the stage with a great deal of flourish, to make a sensational effect, as they do in the parades in Siena, and as Goltzius' flag-bearer appears to be doing; but flags for such a purpose need to be made of a light material, and to put heraldic or ornamental devices upon them with paint would tend to make them unsuitably heavy. To avoid this they would have to be painted with dyes, or sewn together from different coloured pieces of similar fabric, or embroidered. All or any of this could certainly be done, but Elizabethan plays as a rule did not hold the stage for continuous runs, and it is questionable how much a company could be prepared to spend on such elaborate detail at any one time. Even so, in the three *Henry VI* plays the personal heraldry of the great families represented on the stage could not be entirely disregarded by an audience which included lawyers and gentlemen perhaps as many again as the commoners of the yard, who themselves would

81

not be ignorant of the origins of the more famous heraldic devices, such as the red and white roses of York and Lancaster, or of the three suns which appear in the sky to the future King Edward IV before the battle of Towton, and were adopted by him into the heraldry of his shield. In fact these legendary origins are represented on the stage in the action of the *Henry VI* plays themselves and so would be expected at some time to be seen displayed in shields and flags. What I think likely is that the playhouse property room would in time have built up a collection of such heraldic devices – especially those of possibly frequent use, such as the lions of England or the lilies of France – with some other 'ordinary' flags, diapered, crossed, striped or quartered, but of no particular allegiance, which might be used generally for parades.

ANTONY AND CLEOPATRA

There is a certain curious relationship between Shakespeare's early historical trilogy of the *King Henry VI* plays, the first of which was staged at the Rose in March 1592 (it is the only dated record for the performance of any of them) and the grand Roman tragedy of his maturity, *Antony and Cleopatra*, which scholars generally agree was composed in 1607 or 1608. We have seen his panoramic system of stage warfare, with its marching and countermarching of drums and colours and its confrontation of these symbolised armies, in *Henry VI*. Fifteen years later in *Antony and Cleopatra* he suddenly revives the system, intending, as it may seem, to amplify the style and widen the scope of his otherwise classically conceived five-act tragedy. Yet such a technique of brief, rapidly re-located military scenes, occurring in quick succession, as are found in *Antony and Cleopatra*, especially in Act 4, are not usually thought consistent with a classical style of drama, and in that context would have been considered by earlier critics an eccentricity in Shakespeare's genius. A concentrated example of the effect may be found in 3.10, with the stage-direction: *Canidius marcheth with his land army one way over the stage, and Taurus the lieutenant of Caesar the other way: After their going in is heard the noise of a Sea fight.* I have attempted to put that sequence together in the diagram shown on p. 83. It is seen as if on the stage of an open public theatre which for the date of this play may be supposed to be the

Text within the illustration:

"Canidius marcheth with his land army one way over the stage..."

"... and Taurus the lieutenant of Caesar the other way..."

"... After their going in is heard the noise of a sea fight."

27 *Antony and Cleopatra*, 3.10. The marching of the armies.

Globe, viewed from behind the tiring-house. Following what we have recently discussed about the minimal composition of stage armies, the reader will be quick to note that the two marching forces represented here are very generously provided with soldiers, for which my excuse must be that at the time I made the drawing I was more concerned with inventing an exciting figuration for two stage armies, than with their likely physical reality. More to the point in criticism here, I now find, is my use of flags, which were the essential symbol of an army in *Henry VI*, but are not mentioned at all in *Antony and Cleopatra*. Instead of drums and colours, *Antony* has, consistently, drums and trumpets. Military sounds and the *noises* of battle are here insistent, as in the noises of a sea-fight, twice mentioned in these stage-directions. I have shown this in my drawing, represented by gunfire, with the use of 'chambers', as explained with my earlier drawing on p. 50. That the warships of Roman times did not fight with any such weapons would have been a merely pedantic point to put before an Elizabethan audience which was still remembering how the Spanish Armada, only a few years earlier, had been held at bay and driven off in one of the greatest naval actions of the age, by the superior gunnery of the English fleet. For them the noise of a fight at sea meant the exciting noise of gunfire, above all else. To this, in my diagram, I have added some drums and trumpets for good measure.

I have now to say that my diagrammatic supposition that this play was in fact ever performed at the Globe is disputable. The earliest record of its performance anywhere dates from 1669, where it is stated in the Lord Chamberlain's records of that time as one of Shakespeare's plays 'formerly acted at the Blackfriars'. The former company of the Chamberlain's Men had been honoured with the title of the King's Men after the accession of James I, and they had taken over an existing 'private' indoor playhouse, the Blackfriars on the City side of the river, which they occupied continually after 1608 and ran in conjunction with their Globe on the south bank. Plays were frequently thereafter transferred from one playhouse to the other, the Blackfriars catering generally for smaller and presumably more elite audiences. Nevertheless the practical scenic arrangements, and particularly those of the tiring-house facade wall, would have been similarly furnished in both theatres. As an example I show here in fig. 28 the complicated 'monu-ment' scene in 4.15 of *Antony and Cleopatra*. I show it as presented at the Globe (at the Blackfriars it would have been essentially the same, though rather more confined in scale) and I show it with two variants of the scenic wall, that is with and without the addition of the central porch-like feature. The scene is a decisive one in helping to calculate the height and use of the upper stage (and in this respect it also refers back to problems which were opened in the previous chapter).

The situation in the play is that Antony, having been defeated in the battle against Caesar, has thrown himself on his sword and is dying. Meanwhile Cleopatra has taken refuge in her 'monument', which we understand to be a fortress-like memorial tomb. She now appears there 'aloft', that is, on the upper stage, with her two handmaidens and other attendants. From the stage below she is told by an officer, Diomedes, that the dying Antony is being brought to her by his guard, and Diomedes bids her to 'look out o'th'other side your monument' where she will see them approaching. In my drawing (figs. a and b) I show two ways in which this scene may be realised. In the first (fig. a) I show the straight scenic wall without any special addition, except for a railing across the central opening of the upper stage, to allow Cleopatra to lean forward more prominently into the scene where necessary. We see a need for this with Diomedes' injunction to 'look out o'th'other side', whereat Cleopatra leaning forward can at once look from one door to the other. In the alternative setting (b) the platform of the upper-stage 'monument' has itself been built forward to give Cleopatra her necessary dominant position. There are no protective railings at the front of this platform, onto which Antony is soon to be hauled up, and from where Cleopatra can of course conveniently look from on side to the other, and see Antony being carried in 'o'th'other side'. Cranford Adams, in his reconstruction of this scene, has suggested that the 'monument' spanned a wider area of the open-fronted upper stage than I have shown, and that for the 'other side' of it Cleopatra could have gone back to an actual theatre window which could be seen on the far side of the tiring-house, thus allowing her to look to the outside of the theatre itself. Ingenious as this is, I think that looking from side to side between the two

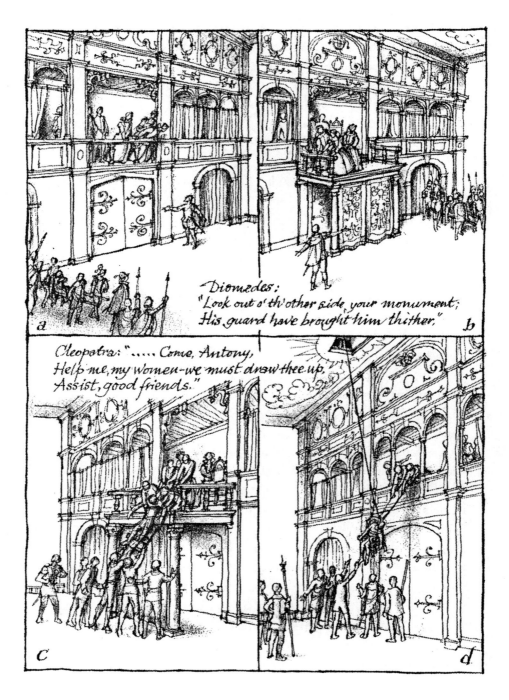

Diomedes:
"Look out o' th' other side, your monument;
His guard have brought him thither."

Cleopatra: "...... Come, Antony,
Help me, my women—we must draw thee up,
Assist, good friends."

28 *Antony and Cleopatra*, 4.15. Two methods of staging.
They heave Antony aloft. Cleopatra's 'monument'.

doors, with Diomedes on one side and the entry of Antony on the other, would serve better.

A more difficult problem now follows. Antony's wounded body has to be hauled to the upper stage so that he may die in Cleopatra's arms. The doing of this is shown in drawings (c) and (d). The height of the upper floor from the stage, allowing reasonable headroom through the stage doors for actors wearing crested helmets and carrying flags and weapons, etc., and for the depth of the upper floor structure itself, can hardly be less than eight feet, and a full-grown, presumably senior actor in armour has to be raised that height from the stage. He can be lifted thus from below by as many men as need be, but from above he has to be hauled in by Cleopatra and her women, that is by boys: 'Help Charmian, help Iras, help: help friends below, let's draw him hither.' In sketch (c) I have supposed the use of the porch without its front railing, thus reducing the up-haul to no more that eight foot six inches (though the sketch makes it look rather higher) and I have supposed that with a rope passed down and under his armpits for hauling, and several men to thrust him up from below he could be drawn without much difficulty to the upper stage. However, if he had to clear the additional height of a balustrade, and certainly if there were an arcade of window-posts in the way, as I have shown (with deliberate unhelpfulness) in my drawing at (d), some additional help would be needed. It has been suggested by Professor Hosley that the overhead crane apparatus sometimes used for the effects of divinities descending from The Heavens ceiling over the stage, might have been used to help with this hoisting. I show the effect of this in my sketch (d). If the crane here were positioned further forward from the tiring-house wall it might also be combined with the porch effect, and would thus be better. But this might all be needlessly elaborate to handle, and given a choice I think I should opt for the solution in sketch (c).

29 *All's Well That Ends Well*, 4.1. Parolles ambushed.

CHAPTER SIX

THE STAGE POSTS AND THEIR USES

·

ALL'S WELL THAT ENDS WELL;
MUCH ADO ABOUT NOTHING;
LOVE'S LABOUR'S LOST (1);
OTHELLO (1)

It was surely by only the slenderest of chances that Johannes de Witt, after his visit to the Swan playhouse in 1596, should have thought to draw a sketch of the place and send it to his friend Arendt van Buchel overseas in Flanders; and that van Buchel should then have copied the sketch into his own note-book; and that the notebook should have survived in darkness for nearly three hundred years, to be found and published by Karl Gaedertz in 1888. With that publication there emerged for the first time the vision, impossible for scholars of an earlier time to conceive, of a theatre with two classically ornate pillars standing widely apart but side by side in the middle of the stage, a thing never seen, imagined, or even reasonably imaginable with any theatre before, yet which have now become so commonly accepted as part of the image of the Shakespearean theatre that it is hard to imagine it without them. In this century the study and architectural analysis of that theatre has explained and justified them, and a further examination of Shakespeare's dramatic style has suggested ingenious and useful ways by which his actors could get around them – for nobody can suggest that they were not some-what in the way – by absorbing them, as they stood, into the action of the plays. In this chapter I shall try to illustrate some examples. (Perhaps not surprisingly they seem to work best with the style of comedy.)

Let me take up again with *All's Well That Ends Well*, from the last chapter. The illustration on p. 88 is from 4.1, and it shows a characteristic combination of modes in Elizabethan staging. The braggart Parolles is addressing his audience directly with a stand-up comic monologue about a significant drum that had been captured by the enemy, which he has bragged he will himself recapture from them: but 'What the devil should move me to undertake the recovery of it, being not ignorant of the impossibility, and knowing I had no such purpose: I must give myself some hurts, and say I got them in exploit . . .' Meanwhile one of his own company, 'with five or six other soldiers in ambush', intending to expose Parolles' poltroonery, have taken up positions in hiding, 'behind this hedge corner'. The 'hedge corner' may be what you will, a painted property-piece carried on, or else some convenient recess or corner of the tiring-house front, or indeed any other thing designated by the speaker, depending upon the place of performance. But in a public playhouse one or both of the stage posts, so often conventionally used for hiding behind, must at once suggest themselves, and so I have adopted them here. Justification will emerge with further instances. Meanwhile in this one, a party in ambush, having listened to Parolles' craven words from behind their 'hedge-corner' posts, are now creeping out upon him. The comic conventionality of the whole scene is established by the fact that while their continuous commentary upon his words can be heard by all the audience as they approach him, Parolles suspects nothing. 'I would I had any drum of the enemies,' he says, 'I would swear I recovered it'. 'You shall hear one anon,' is the approaching comment. 'A drum now of the enemies', he repeats, with emphasis, and at once, with the stage direction *Alarum within*, there comes a violent tattoo beaten upon a drum as his captors seize and bind him.

MUCH ADO ABOUT NOTHING

Perhaps the most famous 'overhearing' scene in classical English comedy is in 2.3 of *Much Ado About Nothing* where Benedick is persuaded, by over-hearing his friends' conversation (they knowing well that he is listening) that Beatrice is in love with him. Benedick, previously on the stage alone, seeing the others approaching, has said 'I will hide me in the arbour'. But they have

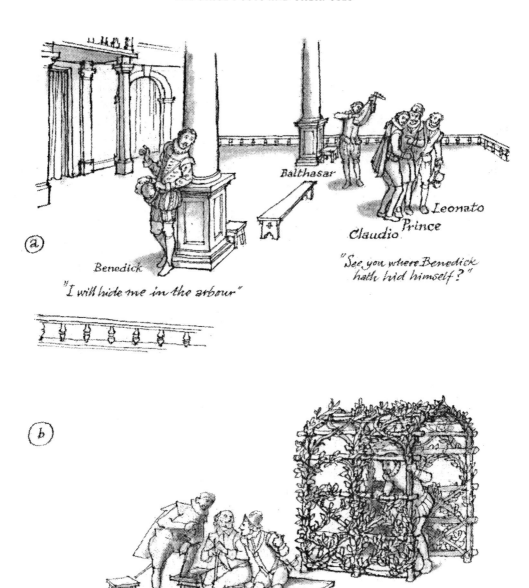

30 *Much Ado About Nothing*, 2.3. Alternative stagings for Benedick's arbour.

noticed his move, ('See you where Benedick hath hid himself?'), and shortly proceed to engage his overhearing, with talk to catch him. I have shown the scene on p. 91 as set in alternative ways, for two different acting places: (a) for a public playhouse with its familiar posts, and (b) for an indoor 'private' theatre such as the Blackfriars, which had no such posts, or for a performance at court or in a nobleman's hall. (The play had continued in popularity since its first appearance in 1598, and in its own day could have been revived and transferred frequently between the Globe and the Blackfriars.)

In my first example, (a), the whole comic mechanism of the scene on both sides is clearly exposed to the audience, and the actors may do as they please with it: it is in their hands to conjure up their own surroundings, 'arbour' and all. In (b) something to represent an arbour will have to be specially provided. The arbour I show here is suggested by a contemporary woodcut illustration on the title-page to Kyd's *The Spanish Tragedy*. As a stage property it is light and easy to manipulate; and I have, while I was about it, tried to make a fine thing of it. Possibly I have gone too far: a mere leafy screen might have served just as well. But the point here is, which of the two methods, for the actors, would be the better? I think there might be a choice in favour of those 'obstructive' posts.

(The character Balthasar seen tuning his lute in fig. a is the Company's boy singer and musician, whose real name, Jack Wilson, has been accidentally entered into the First Folio text at this point, in place of his name in the play. The action is here interrupted while he sings the song 'Sigh No More, Ladies' for us. Such accidents as this, of a real person's name caught into the old text like a fly in amber, are among the incidental attractions of Shakespearean theatre studies.)

In the next act of the play (3.3) the posts are again brought into use for the same purpose, or so I interpret it in my drawing on p. 93. I show the whole stage in a Globe theatre formed with the familiar features of the Swan. The date here may be supposed around 1600. The scene opens with the broad comedy of Constable Dogberry setting his watchmen to their duties. He leaves them to be 'vigitant' in their duties, which, at his departure, they interpret as 'sit we here upon the church bench till two, and then all to bed'. But no such luck for them: there enter Conrad and Borachio to

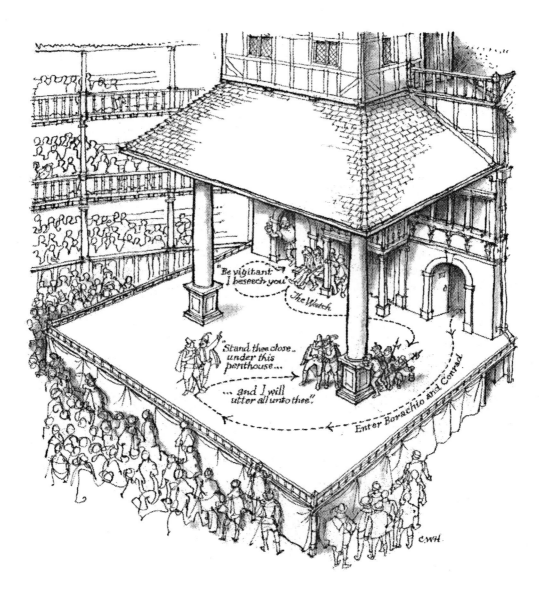

31 *Much Ado About Nothing*, 3.3. Conrad and Borachio overheard by the Watch.

93

the scene, whom the Watch rightly guess to be villains, for them to keep their eyes and ears upon. It is supposed to be very dark and Borachio calls to Conrad to come near, for he has something to tell him. He says further 'Stand thee close under this penthouse, for it drizzles rain, and I will, like a true drunkard, utter all unto thee'. The immediate question arises for us: what and where is 'this penthouse'? In my drawing we may see two possible places. One is the little 'porch' against the tiring-house wall between the two doors. The watchmen are in fact already seated there close by, on the 'church bench', in a good position to overhear the villainy of Borachio's narrative; but it is very far back, not so good as at first it seems, for the whole audience has to hear what must be simulated as a low-spoken confidence. I have preferred to suppose that the two blackguards come out and begin their scene on the forepart of the stage where, as at the Swan, the stage roof has not extended and where if in fact 'it drizzles rain' the actors might in fact get wet. Thus the stage roof itself is the 'penthouse', and when Conrad and Borachio move back under it they come up to 'stand close' against one of the pillars. In the meanwhile, to overhear them better, the watchmen have crept forward (and it's not hard to imagine with what a deal of comic business) into a cluster behind the same pillar and behind each other, from where at the proper moment they can all rush out and pounce upon the villains. This comic 'vigitance', with its supposed pitch darkness and use of lanterns by broad daylight in the afternoon, must surely have much in its favour – and in favour of this use of the stage posts also.

LOVE'S LABOUR'S LOST

A further example of the comedy of hiding and overhearing with the stage posts may be deduced from an analysis of the action in 4.3 of *Love's Labour's Lost*, as illustrated on p. 96. The story situation is that the young King of Navarre and his three close companions, Berowne, Longaville and Dumaine, have vowed together to make 'a little Academe' of their court life, devoting themselves to an elegant bachelorhood of study, and the avoidance of women, for a period of three years. This project is quickly made very difficult for them by the arrival of a diplomatic mission of witty young women, the Princess of France and, likewise, her own three companions, with whom the avowed bachelors of the Academe quickly fall in love, a fall which of course they are obliged to conceal from each other. The exposure of their inevitable failure occurs in 4.3 the scene of my drawing in fig. 32 and, as I show it, again with the prominent help of the two posts.

First on the scene is the wittily cynical monitor of this Academe, Berowne, for whom a failure in these circumstances is not beyond expectation; and so he reflects upon it. He then steps hurriedly aside as he sees the King (Navarre) approaching, with a poem in his hand, sighing, 'Ay me!'. As I show the movements that follow, Berowne who has till now been at stage centre, quickly retreats to hide behind the right-hand post, while Navarre takes his place at the centre (diagram 1). Navarre's self-revelation of love is now likewise interrupted by the arrival of Longaville, in his similar predicament, to whom Navarre now gives up the centre, quickly dodging away to the left-hand post (2). Longaville likewise is interrupted by the love-obsessed Dumaine, from whom he too, dodges away, this time towards the post on the right; but this hiding place has been already occupied by Berowne, who has from there been giving us a commentary upon all these revelations, throughout. Now, however, as Longaville, approaches he in turn gives place and scuttles off (4), of course somehow unseen by Longaville, back into the tiring-house. From there a few moments later he appears at a centre window of the upper stage. 'All hid, all hid', he says, 'an old infant play,/ Like a demi-god, here sit I in the sky. . .' We may, if we choose imagine that he has climbed a tree, and that the two posts have been other trees in the park, for Navarre, when he emerges from his hiding place, says that he has been 'closely shrouded in this bush'. Of course all this comical hiding and overhearing could be, and possibly sometimes was, done by an arrangement of property trees carried on and off at suitable times; but I question whether that would have been any more suitable, or even as funny as these simple manoevres of scurrying from pillar to post could be, and certainly it would have been more cumbersome to stage.

Useful, splendid and even funny as these famous posts may have been, however, there still remains the problem of their outstanding obstructiveness in this circular auditorium. In the imagination we may normally view them more or less from the front, as I show them in many drawings herein,

32 *Love's Labour's Lost*, 4.3. Dumaine overheard all round.

and one can then more or less 'upstage' them as they stand. But what if they are seen from another position? A large part of an Elizabethan audience was listening to the play from more oblique positions, round at the side. The privately-hired 'gentlemen's rooms' would appear to have been located, like the stage-boxes of a nineteenth-century proscenium theatre, at the sides of the stage close to the tiring-house, from which at some theatres privileged patrons were allowed to enter and take their places, even, as we learn from Thomas Dekker[1], upon the stage itself; and we have already seen with our example from *The Taming of the Shrew* that a 'lords' room' could be located actually above and behind the stage. Thus we have for our purposes here to accustom ourselves to a different view of playgoing and even of seeing the plays. I cannot leave a discussion of the stage posts, therefore, without attempting to show their effect when seen from a side position. The scene I have chosen is from *King Henry IV, Part One*, 5.4. (p. 98). I have perhaps chosen a favourable example because it is a scene of action at the battle of Shrewsbury, where with so much movement the posts cannot obscure the view of much of it all of the time. In this case there are forays and combats back and forth, as here of Prince Hal with Hotspur. Their fight is observed and cheered on by Falstaff from a safe distance (probably behind a pillar) until: *Enter Douglas, he fights with Falstaff, who falls down as if he were dead.* Falstaff later observes, Douglas having thankfully departed, that 'the better part of valour is Discretion'.

In this chapter I have been describing some of the ways in which the two stage posts might have been put to dramatic use, under the general supposition that they were always something of an acceptable inconvenience. In terms of a modern theatre, that of course can hardly be denied. Yet we should consider also that for Elizabethan audiences they would certainly have been less of a nuisance than we imagine. The Elizabethans paid for admission not to any fixed position in the auditorium, but to an area; so if in a gallery one found oneself on a bench behind a post one could usually work one's way around to somewhere better. In the yard below there would be a

---

1 Thomas Dekker, *The Gull's Hornbook* (1608), chapter 6, 'How a Gallant should behave himself in a Play-house.'

33 *The First Part of King Henry IV*, 5.4. Falstaff in battle. ('The betterpart of valour is Discretion . . .').

certain amount of movement among the groundlings all the time, and I imagine the immovable stage posts would have been one of the causes of this. A convenient view of the stage was something the Elizabethan playgoer had continually to arrange for himself.

CHAPTER SEVEN

STAGE BEDS AND
OTHER FURNITURE

·

OTHELLO (2);
THE SECOND PART OF KING HENRY VI (2)
THE FIRST AND SECOND PARTS OF
KING HENRY IV

We may suppose that most Elizabethan plays were furnished on the stage from a single stock of utilitarian pieces always on hand in the tiring-house: one or two tables, some stools and benches, and a few grand pieces such as thrones for royal occasions, brought out time and again and recognised as familiar friends by all regular playgoers. If a new special piece were added it would be noted for comparative approval, as it took its place in the repertoire. No one reading this will be surprised by it. But there is one special item in the tiring-house stock to which special attention should be drawn, because its use appears to be unique to the Elizabethan theatre. I can think of no other corpus of dramatic literature or composition which employs this item in such a frequent, familiar and varied manner. It is the Elizabethan stage bed.

Basically it appears to have been used in two different ways. Sometimes it occupies a fixed position behind curtains, such as the central 'discovery space' of the tiring-house frontage. I have shown this in my drawings for *Romeo and Juliet* (chapter 3, above), as where Juliet *falls on her bed within the curtains*. But there are many other cases, not only in Shakespeare but throughout the corpus of Elizabethan/Jacobean drama as a whole, where the bed is mobile, brought out from the tiring-house onto the main stage and taken back again as required. In *The Second Part of King Henry IV* we have the simple stage-management direction 'Bed put forth', with in this case the murdered body of the Duke of Gloucester exhibited upon it (see fig. 36). Such references to beds 'thrust out' are numerous. A favourite example is from Middleton's comedy *A Chaste Maid In Cheapside* which has: *A bed thrust out upon the stage: Allwit's wife in it.* A group of Mrs Allwit's woman friends have come to visit her, and they sit around her bed gossiping. One must suppose that the visibility and stage management of beds in either case, fixed or mobile, could be made satisfactory for the audience all around in the theatre to hear and see the action, and a classic example must be with the dramatic management of Desdemona's bed in *Othello*.

Here it is necessary to pause a moment, to examine the picturesque claims of an established old friend, the familiar Elizabethan 'four-poster bed'. Because it appears to be an integrated structural unit, already furnished with its necessary curtains, it has sometimes been supposed by scholars that this was the kind of bed Shakespeare had in mind when he was writing the final act of his great play. If so we should suppose that a 'four-poster', or some manageably modified form of it, was thrust out from the tiring-house onto the stage, and that in those terrible moments during the murder when Aemilia is knocking at the door and Othello draws the curtains across the fatal bed, that these of course would be the curtains of a four-poster unit. In fact, that is unlikely. Such beds in Shakespeare's time usually needed only *two* posts. The overhead 'tester' which carried the curtains was usually attached either to the wall, or sometimes to a large headboard at the head end of the bed; and at the other it was supported by its two posts which stood directly upon the floor, not attached to the bed but only to the tester above. This created a curtained enclosure within which the bed itself was fitted as a separate thing. From these parts in later times the 'four-poster' bed was devised, by joining them all together into one moveable piece. The sumptuous four-poster beds now to be seen in museums or historic country-houses are of a later date, usually from the Restoration period or later. With this in mind we may now return to Desdemona's bedchamber in *Othello*; though it may be more interesting to enter it not directly but by way of the previous scene, thus linking it also to the subject of our previous chapter, those other two great posts standing upon the stage.

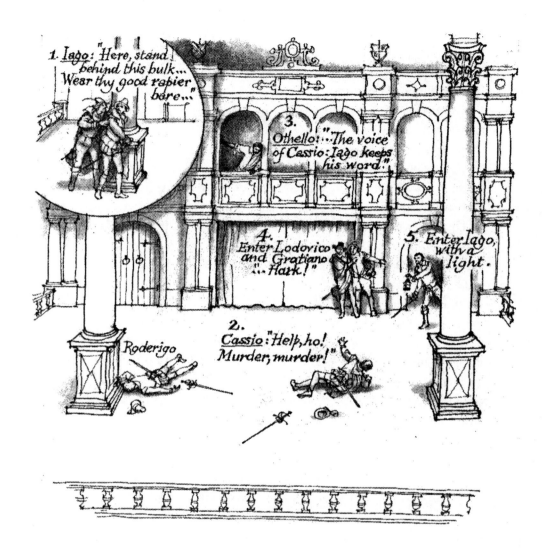

34 *Othello*, 5.1. The wounding of Cassio (as at the Globe).

I read that the composition of *Othello* can be dated fairly closely, around the year 1604. It was then acted at the Globe theatre and later at the Blackfriars, after the Chamberlain's/King's Men had taken occupation of that playhouse also, in 1608. My illustrations here (figs. 34 and 35) show it as enacted at each of these theatres. The first is at the Globe, with its two pillars, one of which, as shown in the inset, is used for Roderigo to hide behind in his bungled attempt to murder Cassio. The clue for this, in the text, is Iago's hurried instruction to him: 'Here, stand behind this bulk, straight will he come'. We must in this case allow that at the Globe 'this bulk' is most likely to have been one of the stage pillars, nothing else being so opportune for the purpose. Then in the turmoil that follows, with the wounding of Cassio, the death of Roderigo, the flight and return of Iago, and Cassio's calling for help, there comes the sudden and awkward stage direction: *Enter Othello*. Awkward, because difficult to place. Othello has no part in all the scurry on the stage: he is there only to comment, which he cannot do effectively if he has to do it at stage level only by looking out of a door or round a corner. Just as we have taken the liberty of interpreting the 'bulk' as a stage-post, in this case I feel most strongly that the stage-direction for Othello's entry at this point is incomplete: it should read *Enter Othello above*. I have shown him 'above' in my drawing, and I hope it demonstrates convincingly that by this simple use of one of the typical built-in conventions of the Shakespearean theatre the action on the stage is not made more confused but is in fact completed, and the drama is pushed further towards its awful conclusion. Othello, from his window above, relishes what he thinks is the beginnings of his revenge: 'Iago keeps his word' . . . 'O brave Iago, honest and just, that hast such noble sense of thy friend's wrong . . . Minion, your dear lies dead . . . Strumpet, I come. . .' And thus deluded he leaves the scene, passing along the gallery towards Desdemona's bedchamber. This I show in fig. 35 as done at the indoor Blackfriars theatre (where I think the smaller space and more enclosed feeling of the place may have been more suitable to this play than the wide and open Globe). I show two alternative methods for the presentation of Desdemona's bed. Method (a) shows the bed positioned in the central 'discovery space' of the backstage frontage, as for Juliet's bed (which becomes her tomb) discussed above in chapter 3:

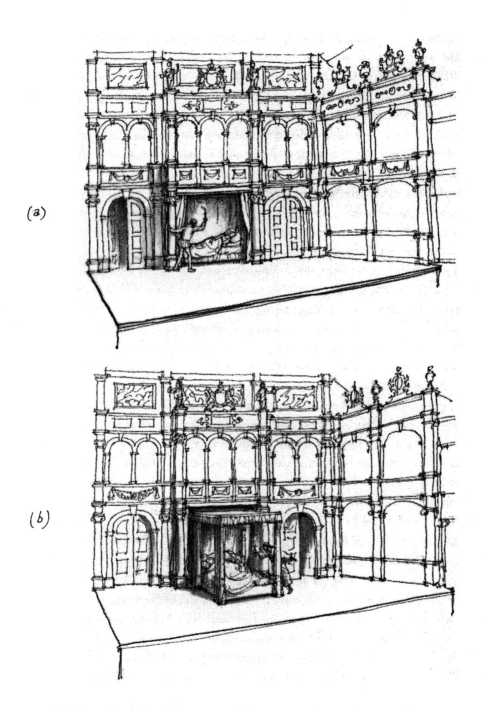

35 *Othello*, 5.2. Two methods for staging Desdemona's bed (as at the Blackfriar's Theatre).

only in this instance I have supposed a design in which the whole centre part of the frontage stands forward by a little over one foot from the rest, thus giving the bed (or any other use of the discovery-space) a little more prominence. Method (b) shows the bed with the greatest possible prominence, being thrust out from backstage into the stage's centre, bringing its dramatically necessary curtains with it, four-poster fashion. I have to say I see no advantage in this. The posts and curtains seem to me equally if not more obstructive to dramatic action and visibility by this method than they are with the comparative 'upstaging' of Method (a), to say nothing of the cumbersome business of bringing the bed on stage from its encumbering backstage storage. But let me leave it thus, as a problem needing trial by practice, while I pass on to another example wherein both methods are nicely used in one play.

We have already had reference to the stage-direction 'Bed put forth' in the *Second Part of King Henry VI* and the illustration for it given here in fig. 36 a. For this play I have employed the practical variant of a discovery space which I feel could, should or must have been used at least sometimes in some theatres, and which I have used fairly widely among illustrations herein: the prow-like addition to the upper stage, thrust forward about two or three feet from the backstage facade and carried on two posts at the front. It is here hung around with curtains, from which in this case (3.2) the bed is 'put forth', as I show, with the dead body of Duke Humfrey of Gloucester upon it. But we should now note that the direction 'put forth' is taken from the 1623 First Folio version of the play. There is a much earlier (First Quarto) version dated from 1594, possibly concurrent with a presentation at the Rose theatre, which has it very differently: *Then the Curtains being drawn, Duke Humfrey is discovered in his bed, and two men lying on him and smothering him in his bed.* The curtains are then evidently closed again, for later on we have another direction: *Warwick draws the curtains and shows Duke Humfrey in his bed.* Of course at different times and in different theatres we may expect things differently done, the bed 'discovered' in one case and 'thrust forth' in another. At the earlier theatre of 1594 it seems they favoured the discovery method, for in the same Quarto version of the play a little further on we have another dramatic bed scene: '. . . *and then the Curtains be drawn,*

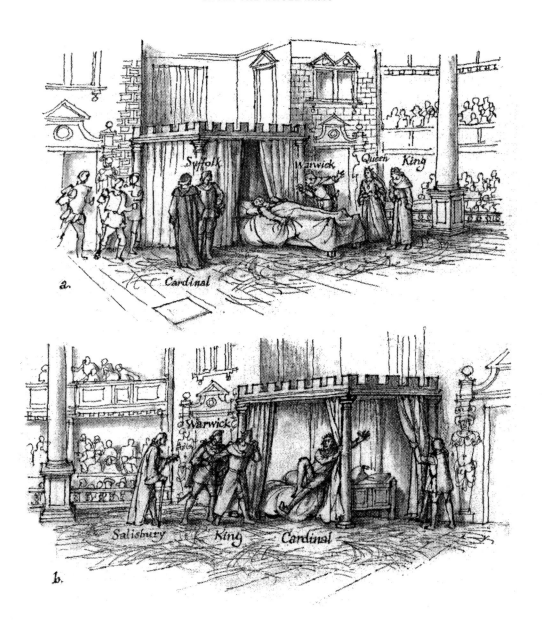

36 *The Second Part of King Henry VI.* The staging of bed scenes
(a) 3.2, *Bed put forth*; (b) 3.3 Bed *discovered*.

and the Cardinal is discovered in his bed, raving and staring as if he were mad'. I show this scene in my sketch (b) in fig. 36. When I first drew the two scenes on this page I had the idea that, with two similar but different incidents coming so near together in the play there would have been an attempt to differentiate them visually as much as possible, and so I did this myself, making the bed 'thrust forth' in one scene, and 'discovered' in the other. It was mildly ingenious of me, but, as I now find, wrong: the earlier version, concurrent with the date of the Rose, uses the discovery method all through, while the thrusting-out method may be a usage from some other, probably larger, playhouse. Certainly the small compass of the Rose, even after Henslowe's enlargement of it in 1592, was one of the most important surprises revealed by the excavation of its foundations in 1989. I am here tempted by it to risk another guess. It is possible that the small size of the Rose and its stage, with the presumably cramped conditions of its backstage area and the comparative closeness of the audience all around, were in fact more favourable to the 'discovery' method, with its curtains, than to the pushing around of a space-cumbering object such as a bed (even allowing that that is unlikely to have been a four-poster). A movable bed thrust out onto the open mid-stage would be better used and better seen in the larger theatres from which most of its relevant stage-directions derive.

Perhaps the most notable dramatic use of the 'putting forth' of a bed in any Shakespeare play has in fact no actual stage-direction to that effect in the text at all. It occurs in Act 4 of *King Henry IV, Part Two*, where there is a most evident change of scene on the open stage while the line of action continues uninterruptedly with all the same characters remaining on the stage and no *Exeunt* given for them between one scene and the next. In the First Folio text it is all given as an undivided part of 'Actus Quartus, Scena Secunda'. The action is that Henry IV is suddenly taken ill. His heir, Prince Henry, is not present, as his three brothers are, and the king asks anxiously about him. Then he says: 'My brain is giddy, Oh me, come near me, I am much ill. . . . I pray you take me up and bear me hence / Into some other chamber. . . .' Here the scene evidently divides. The king almost at once is found to be in his bed, and he says: 'Set me the Crown upon my pillow here'. There is soft music offstage. On stage with the king are the Earl of Warwick and the three younger princes, to whom now the heir, Prince Henry enters, and the stage is set towards the famous scene of his taking possession of the crown, and his dialogue with his father.

Analysing this classic puzzle of Elizabethan staging I find that if only we allow it to be done with a movable bed, it is after all simpler than it seems. In my diagrams on pages 109 and 110 I offer a solution in two different ways. In the first method (fig. 37) I have numbered the incidents of the action in sequence. In the upper picture we see the king taken ill in his chair (1). The chair is fitted for carrying with poles, which I have thoughtfully provided with two attendant carriers on the left of the picture; and so, upon the king's asking to be borne 'hence, into some other chamber' the poles are quickly fitted and he is lifted. 'Hence', however, as we see, is not far, and while he is carried only a short way around the stage, his bed (2) is thrust forward from behind the curtained opening at the back, and he is lifted into it. So the scene has changed without a break, and Prince Henry now enters it at the door marked (3). The action continues in the lower sketch (where I now think it would be better if the king's bed had been brought and stationed further forward than I show it here). At (4) the princes and the Earl of Warwick leave the scene, while Prince Henry remains to watch at the sleeping king's bedside, where also on the pillow sits the crown ('O polished perturbation, golden Care!') which the Prince, whom I here indicate as moving round and perhaps pausing at the back of the bed, so that for a moment we can see the king, the prince and the crown all grouped closely together. Prince Henry then takes up the crown and brings it down to centre stage at (5) where he puts it on his own head (unless perhaps the words 'Lo, here it sits . . .' may be addressed to the crown still in its place on the pillow).

The cycle of changes from one room to another, which is dramatically important for the irony later to be revealed, is now complete; but there is one other way of staging this continuous scene which may be as good, or perhaps even preferable. Being myself unable to decide about it, I offer it here briefly, as an alternative, at fig. 38 on p. 110. At (1) the king in his chair is carried, not to another position on the stage as in the previous method, but straight off stage by one of the two doors. The bed is then brought forward onto the stage as before (2). The king is then brought back to the stage by the other

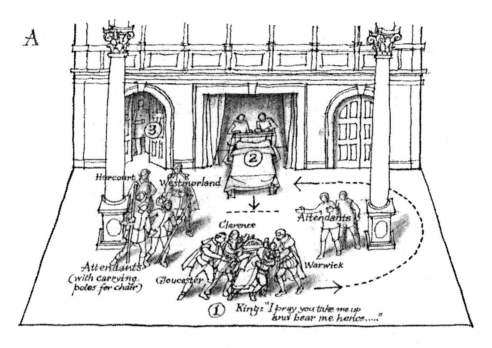

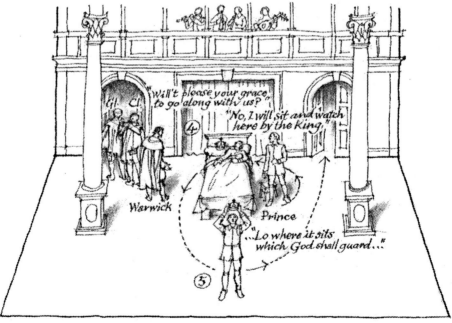

37 *The Second Part of King Henry IV*, 4.5. The king falls sick and is taken 'into some other chamber'.
Method A of managing the change of scene.

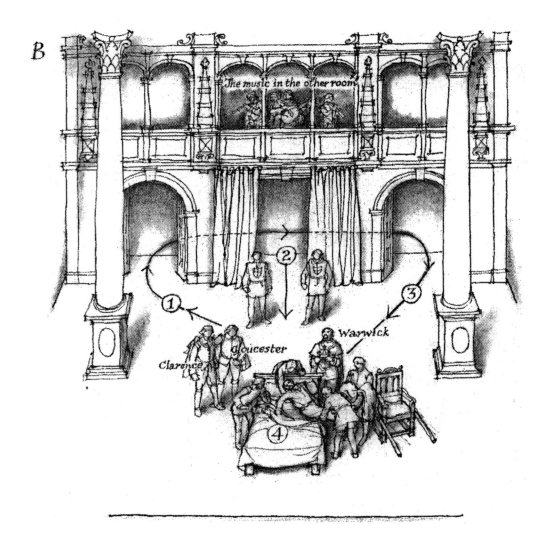

38 *The Second Part of Henry IV*, 4.5. The king falls sick and is taken 'into some other chamber'. Method B of managing the change of scene.

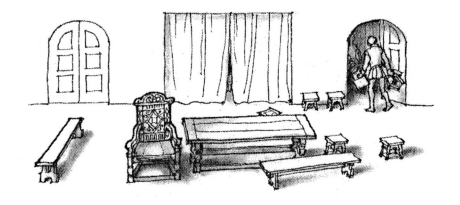

39 *The First Part of King Henry IV.* Scenic positions of basic stage furniture.

door (3) and transferred to his bed. Warwick is here shown holding the king's crown, which has fallen from his head. The ironical motivation for these changes of location lies in the historical tradition which Shakespeare took from Holinshed's Chronicle, that when the king was first taken sick in the abbot's palace at Westminster his attendants 'bare him into a chamber that was next at hand, . . . and used all remedies to revive him'. At length he recovered his speech, and understanding and perceiving himself in a strange place which he knew not, he willed to know if the chamber had any particular name; whereunto answer was made, that it was called Jerusalem. Then said the King: 'Lauds be given to the Father of Heaven, for now I know that I shall die here in this chamber; according to the prophesy of me declared, that I should depart this life in Jerusalem'. And he concludes: 'Which vainly I supposed the Holy Land / But bear me to that chamber, there I'll lie: / In that Jerusalem shall Harry die'.

A stage direction has here called for 'the music in the other room'. In this drawing I show it as at the windows of the upper stage, where indeed it probably would have been played: but I think here it may perhaps have been better unseen, from behind closed curtains.

I finish this chapter with a drawing (fig. 39) of some of the 'Other Furniture' with which it began, here shown in use with four scenes from *Henry IV, Part One*. (1) The tavern in Eastcheap, with Falstaff, crowned with a cushion to parody the king rebuking Prince Hal for the bad company he keeps. (2) The same arrangement, but with the royal crown now set formally upon the table, as representing the palace. The prince accepts his father's rebuke. (3) The map on the table. Hotspur and Glendower contest the divisions of the kingdom. (4) The royal throne on its dais: King Henry's court, with Hotspur.

Of course, besides this store of ordinary furniture, the property room would contain a variety of occasional pieces made for special effects, some of which will appear in the following pages.

40 *The First Part of King Henry VI*, 5.3. Joan La Pucelle deserted by the Fiends.
They hang their heads.

CHAPTER EIGHT

SPECIAL EFFECTS

·

THE FIRST, SECOND AND THIRD PARTS OF HENRY VI (2); HAMLET; MACBETH; PERICLES, PRINCE OF TYRE; THE TEMPEST

To see a play performed on a stage is to watch an artistic apparatus, a living model created to represent a section of human society at some critical moment of its imagined history, demonstrating its aspirations, its comic or tragic fortunes, its hopes and fears. We, the audience, are captivated by it, because in fact a good model can often perform better than the subject in real life, calling upon resources beyond the reach of the daily reality it pretends to be. It can show distant causes and their effects brought together in one time and place. Where there are problems it can create solutions: at special need it can even 'call spirits from the vasty deep' or bring down gods from Heaven to assist. Such extensions of human power, in one form or another, have been a particular feature of the theatre from the most primitive times to the present day. Now, in this age of the cinema, television and video, these marvellous projections are boundlessly widened by the technology of special effects, and can be summoned from the vasty deep into the production script by a stroke of the pen, with the magic formula FX. But (for example) the monsters and 'extra-terrestrials' which are popular frighteners in today's horror films, had their similar counterparts in Shakespeare's theatre wherein, although doubtless they were less ingenious than today's devils; if you only ventured near enough to the stage they could claw you, or fizz you with fireworks and glare you in the eye.

The devils that accompanied Satan and Beelzebub with the Mystery Plays in the towns of medieval England, and dwelt in the Hell underneath the stages of their temporary street theatres, stayed on and took up residence for a while under the stages of the new permanent playhouses, in the cellarage which continued to be known as Hell. They were still there when Shakespeare was working at the Rose theatre, and although as a rule he did not have much use for them, they emerged in the first two parts of his early *King Henry VI* plays. In the first they come up to bring bad news to Joan of Arc. The diabolical powers by which alone she has been enabled to defeat the heroic English are about to leave her. She summons them. The text in the Folio gives *Thunder*, and then *Enter Fiends*. She begs their customary help, but *They walk about and speak not*. At her further entreaties *They hang their heads*, then *They shake their heads*, and finally *They depart*. This, from 5,3, is the scene I show on p. 113, fig. 40. It should be observed that the part of Joan is played by a boy, and so may some if not all of the Fiends.

The fiendish costumes would have been made up in canvas or leather, cut into fish scales and painted black, red or green. The masks and headdresses would have been of leather or moulded parchment. A collection of all these would have been a permanent part of the playhouse wardrobe, and it may be imagined that some items may even have been bought in from the surplus stock of the ancient mystery plays. They were, after all, timeless in their use.

The stage-trap shown here leading up from the Hell by way of a simple flight of steps avoids discussion of the complex mechanisms which were evidently designed and fitted as the playhouses developed their techniques. Thus we have, from a play of 1612[1]: *Flashes of fire; the Divels appear* [i.e. from traps] *at every corner of the stage, with several fireworks*. This seems to indicate no less than four separate traps, with stage-hands to manage them and to help the devil-costumed actors to leap up and out quickly onto the stage. Such traps would need to be very well fitted and securely barred underneath when not in use. Beside these there had also to be a larger trap, presumably in a central position, suitable for a grave, as that for Ophelia in Hamlet 5,1 (fig. 52), into which two actors have to leap down and grapple each other.

---

1 Thomas Heywood, *The Silver Age*, possibly presented at the Rose in 1595.

41 *The Second Part of King Henry VI*, 1.4. The conjuration.
It thunders and lightens terribly: then the Spirit riseth.

The earliest form of trap would presumably have been a simple hinged door opening downwards, but in later times stage carpenters invented a system whereby a trap door could be dipped down to slide aside on horizontal runners just below the stage, while a second trap door, with a person on it, was quickly brought up from below to take its place. Such a sliding device would also have given better room for the use of steps from below, and I show this, with a larger opening which allows for the entry of a whole group of devils together, in my drawing for Joan of Arc from, *Henry VI* on p. 114.

In the second of his three *Henry VI* plays Shakespeare makes an opportunity for another scene with a devil-trap. The occasion (in 1.4) is the suspected conspiracy of Elinor Cobham, Duchess of Gloucester, to use witchcraft against the life of King Henry. As reported in Holinshed's Chronicles, the plot was that the conspirators 'at the request of the said Duchess, had devised an image of wax representing the King, which by their sorcery by little and little consumed; intending thereby in conclusion to waste and destroy the king's person'. This ancient and familiar practice of witchcraft, intended to consume the King's life along with his image, would also have consumed too much time for Shakespeare's dramatic purpose, and he quickly changed it. In its place we have the scene of diabolical conjuration shown here in fig. 41. The persons involved are the necromancer Bullingbrook, two treacherous priests (Southwell and Hume), the witch Margery Jourdain (who is bidden to 'be prostrate and grovel in the earth') and the Duchess herself who is stationed 'aloft'. (In an earlier Quarto version of the play she is given the line 'I will stand upon this tower here', followed by the stage-direction *She goes up to the tower*.) When they are all set, the stage-direction says: *Here do the Ceremonies belonging, and make the Circle. Bullingbrook or Southwell reads* Conjuro te, *etc. It Thunders and Lightens terribly: then the Spirit riseth*. That the spirit is in the form of a devil is made clear when he is dismissed later: 'Descend to darkness and the burning lake. False Fiend, avoid!' Then *Thunder and Lightning. Exit Spirit*.

It is evident that the trap used in this case is fairly small, for a single person only, not for a group, as in the previous example, and it has to be contained within the magic circle drawn on the stage. Therefore it could not have room for an ascent by way of stairs, but must be served with a lifting device or platform, its occupant rising vertically, propelled from beneath probably by mechanical means. We have seen above that there could be several such traps as this, even 'at every corner of the stage'. With the settlement of the profession into permanent theatres, the tricks and carpentry of the trade had developed rapidly. A vertically operated trap would have to be fitted with a flush and level stage-floor opening, which could sink and move aside to allow a second piece of floor to rise smoothly from below, with an actor upon it, and fit neatly into the place of the first: and vice versa.

HAMLET

If I am right in my interpretation of the staging of 1. 4 and 5 in *Hamlet*, a device of this kind was in regular use at the Globe after its opening in 1599. The scene, shown here in fig. 42 is the first meeting between Hamlet and his father's Ghost. The presence of the armoured Ghost in this play is never more impressive than when it is played straight, of itself, without weird lighting, or sound effects to give him a sort of hollow awfulness in his voice. (Worst of all is to make him an amplified voice only, with recorded sound, as if his presence is no more than a figment of the imagination: I have seen it done). But this Ghost is to be majestically seen and believed, and in his two appearances in 1.1 he makes his entries stalking upright around the stage without any supernatural paraphernalia. But I would give him one trick, which I indicate in the drawing (at points 1 and 2). I have supposed that the Ghost enters at one of the two stage doors – in this case on the right – makes a circuit of the stage, passing between Horatio and his friends unchecked, and exits by the other door. But later, when it re-enters ('But soft, behold, look where it comes again') it comes *the same way*, by the right-hand door, makes the same circuit, and goes out again on the left. The effect might be like one of the mechanical figures on an ancient cathedral clock, where at the striking of the hour a line of figures move around in a circle between two openings. Here, in Scene 4, where Hamlet himself comes to encounter his father's Ghost, the same thing happens. The Ghost enters as before on the right and begins his circuit. Encountered by Hamlet he stops and beckons

42 *Hamlet*, 1.4 and 5. Entrances and departures of the Ghost.

him away from his friends. He and Hamlet exit, again on the left, and shortly after both re-enter on the right again and move to centre stage for their dialogue and the Ghost's narration. But after this, with the Ghost's next exit, I suggest there is a difference. There are clear and repeated indications that the Ghost is now present not upon the stage but under it, in the 'cellarage' of the stage Hell. When Horatio and Marcellus enter to Hamlet on the stage, he bids them swear upon the cross of his sword to tell no one what they have heard and seen. They are at first reluctant, but the *Ghost cries under the Stage*: 'Swear!' More than that, Hamlet takes them to different parts of the stage and bids them again to swear, and the Ghost moves underneath with them, crying 'Swear' at each place. All this suggests that after his long scene with Hamlet the Ghost does not exit as before, by a doorway, but – with 'Adieu, adieu, Hamlet: remember me' – sinks directly into the ground. The audience has seen him go down. Without this, but with an ordinary stage-level door exit instead, his voice and subsequent movements under the stage, in the Hell to which he has gone 'unhouseled, disappointed, unanealed', could not, or at least might not, be heard or clearly understood. Certainly there existed a mechanism for making such a descent. Stage-trap work is a theatrical science with a long history of its own. What I show in my drawing is, of course, guesswork. The effect, however, and the presentation surrounding it is I think, sustainable and likely.

MACBETH

The only text of *Macbeth* is that of the First Folio, of 1623, but the play had been popular on the stage for nearly twenty years before that. A performance at King James' court was reported in 1606, and one at the Globe playhouse later in 1611; but in the intervening years there had been many other Globe performances, some with amendments and adaptations which were not always by Shakespeare himself: for instance, the scene in which the witches' goddess Hecate makes her appearance to them in 3.5 is believed to have been written into the script by Middleton to make use of the overhead crane mechanism, above the Heavens ceiling, from which she descends seated in a 'foggy cloud'. In the next Act she appears again, briefly, while the witches are preparing their magic cauldron for the perdition of

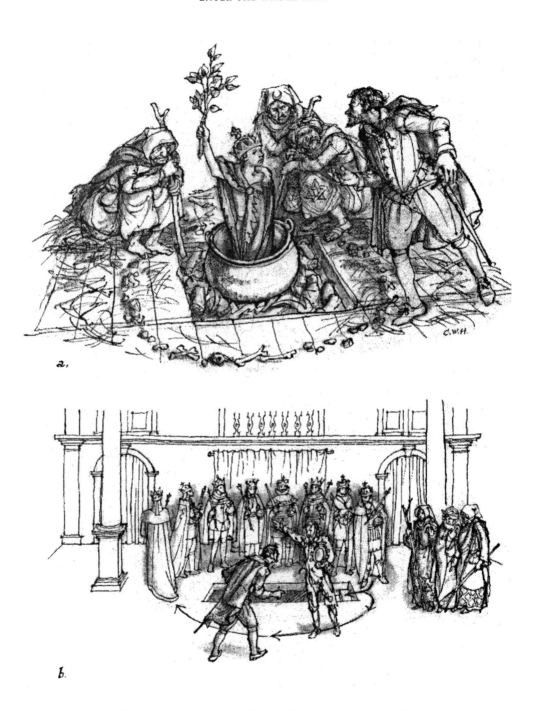

43 *Macbeth*, 4.1. Apparitions (a) The cauldron, with the Crowned Child;
(b) Banquo's Ghost and the show of eight kings.

Macbeth. That cauldron and the trap work associated with it suggest that it is certainly no ordinary cooking pot, with its 'fire burn and cauldron bubble'; and it is unlikely that the stage-hands had the toil and trouble of carrying it and putting it in position in the centre of the stage, where undoubtedly it would have been set. It would have had to have been a large vessel about two feet in diameter. A stage-direction calls for thunder as the witches enter, and, as the cannon-balls rumble and bump impressively along the thunder-run in The Heavens overhead, the central portion of a large trap opens in the stage and the cauldron emerges from it, possibly upon a bed of smoking peat and logs. Smoke, not heat, is what is needed, and that only to start with, for this cauldron is open at the bottom below the stage, and the three apparitions, an *Armed Head*, a *Bloody Child*, and a *Child Crowned with a Tree in his hand* will in turn rise up in it at the witches' command to confront Macbeth. This I show in fig. 43, sketch (a). The crowned child represents Banquo's descendants, the royal house of Scotland, and the tree is a forecast of Birnam Wood, the shadowy trees with which all Macbeth's ambitions are to be overthrown. He demands of the witches to show him the future: they demur at first, but he insists, and then he asks: 'Why sinks that cauldron?'

The crowned child in the cauldron has already 'descended': now the cauldron itself sinks into the stage. The answer to Macbeth's question, why does it do so, lies not in the narrative, but in the stagecraft. The witches are about to present Macbeth with 'a show of eight kings', who are Banquo's successors. There is solemn music for them as they enter. It might be supposed that they should enter at one of the two doors, make a circuit of the stage and go out at the other, following the path suggested previously for the Ghost in *Hamlet*; but evidently this was not so here. The eight kings are summoned up from below, and the cauldron has to sink and be removed to make way for them and a flight of steps. At the same time, I suggest, the trap, which so far had been wide enough only for a cauldron, as in sketch (a), has now to be further widened to allow the kings to come with dignity up the flight of stairs (for they must march upright all the way). That they come from below is indicated by Macbeth's greeting to the first of them: 'Thou art too like the spirit Banquo: Down!' – meaning, we must suppose, to be back whence he came. I show a modest version of what must have been an excit-ing scene in sketch (b), with the bloody ghost of Banquo pointing to the line of his successors. In this drawing Banquo is himself holding the glass in which Macbeth sees Banquo's lineage stretching out 'to the crack of Doom'. Banquo and the procession of kings then descend from the stage and the trap closes over them. The witches summon up music and make to cheer Macbeth's 'sprights' with a grotesque dance. Then, says the text, they 'vanish'.

A schematic diagram showing the operation of the basic mechanical effects available in the public playhouses in the 1590s and after, is given on p. 125.

Having examined some uses of the traps down to the 'cellarage' of Hell, we should now turn to its opposite, the descent from Heaven. We may assume that this was always a very popular effect, at least among the com-moner sort of playgoers, but direct references to it as seen in action in the theatres are rare, and its use has to be imagined more than a little by com-monsensical interpretation. For example, when discussing Hecate's visita-tion to the witches in *Macbeth* just now, I described her as descending seated in 'a foggy cloud': In fact that was perhaps pushing the evidence rather far. This interpretation of her entrance is based a combination of acceptances: first, that her scenes are believed all to have been put into the play by (prob-ably) Middleton for the specific purpose of using the mechanical flying effect, which seems not to have been much favoured by Shakespeare himself; next she is a goddess of the moon, and describes herself as having much magic work in hand up there, to which she must quickly return; and lastly, in going, she says 'I am for the air', adding 'Hark, I am called, my little spirit, see,/sits in a foggy cloud and waits for me'. We may thus assume that the flying device, presumably in the form of a throne, is waiting for her at stage level; therefore, that it has already descended, and therefore again that she had come down in it; and further that it is dressed in such a way that it may be described as 'a foggy cloud' – we may perhaps suppose that it was set in a scenic frame, painted and cut out to simulate clouds; and lastly, unless the 'little spirit' was merely something painted on the cloudy background, that it was capable of carrying two persons, one of whom was small and young,

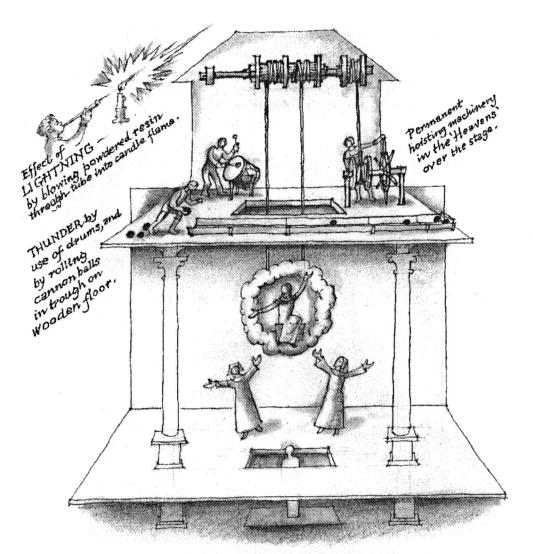

Effect of
LIGHTNING —
by blowing powdered resin
through tube into candle flame.

THUNDER by
use of drums, and
by rolling
cannon balls
in trough on
wooden floor.

Permanent
hoisting machinery
in the 'Heavens'
over the stage.

Stage trap for graves, ghosts
apparitions, etc.

44 Diagram of generally available stage machinery and special effects.

and had the task of steadying the apparatus while Hecate seated herself in it, and then when all was ready, signalling to those above for the ascent. But with all this we must of course recognise what a great deal of speculation has now been propagated from a very few scraps of original evidence. True enough; but if those scraps are themselves firm and sound (as they are) we should also ask, how else can they be interpreted? There seems no sensible alternative.

Evidence for the throne or chair descending from the Heavens is plentiful throughout Elizabethan stage literature. A favourite early example, much quoted, is from Robert Greene's *Alphonsus of Aragon*, of 1587, a play which ends with the stage-direction: *Exit Venus. Or if you conveniently can, let a chair come down from the top of the stage and draw her up.* In the years after this, however, there was no further uncertainty about convenience, for the 'creaking throne' which came down 'the boys to please', as Ben Jonson disdainfully described it, in the Prologue of his *Every Man in His Humour*, had quickly been fitted up in every theatre that could take one. The evidence for this has been extensively examined by Professor Adams.[2]

Jonson's 'creaking Throne' is of course a compelling piece of first-hand evidence from a writer who knew his subject intimately, but perhaps we ought not to let it pass entirely without question: What, we may ask, is this matter about its creakiness? Of course, the mere mention of such a fault in this case is part of the convincingness of the evidence itself. Nevertheless we know that it was Jonson's particular concern to use the theatre as a place for exposing the foibles and 'humours' of human society – the way of the world – and he had little use for its painted mechanical playthings. The creakiness of his throne may thus have derived more from a distaste for the whole apparatus, than from the carpentry of it. A nation of skilled timber-framers and shipwrights, given also a little axle-grease, might have been expected to install a windlass in a theatre without it creaking too audibly. (However, Professor Adams and others have pointed out that in most plays where there is a stage-direction for the use of the flying throne, this is usually accompa-

---

2 John Cranford Adams, *The Globe Playhouse* (Harvard University Press, 1943). A seminal work which, although now outdated in some of its conclusions, is still as inspiring as when it first appeared.

nied by a cue for music or thunder. These would naturally increase the awe and splendour of the divine descent: But the suggestion is that they might also serve to cover the creaks.)

Like Jonson, Shakespeare as a playwright did not have much use for antique divinities descending to the stage in thrones; but as a managing member of the company that owned the Globe playhouse, with the throne and all its hoisting gear ready, installed in The Heavens and waiting to be used, he would not be strongly opposed to using it, given an occasion; and the first occasion seems to have been with *Macbeth*. King James, soon after his accession, had honoured the Chamberlain's Men with his personal patronage: from now on they were to be called the King's Men. In due course, therefore, their most noted playwright responded to the Scottish King and his court, with a Scottish play, *Macbeth*. A prominent and very topical feature of the play, recognising the King's fear and hatred of the evils of witchcraft, was the element of black magic in it, with the three witches, the bubbling cauldron and 'the gruel thick and slab'. After its first presentation with a Court performance in 1606, the play soon established itself as a favourite at the Globe, with frequent revivals and revisions, which may have included additions to the ever-popular scenes of witchcraft, additions which Shakespeare must have approved even if he did not write them all himself. I think it likely that the Hecate scenes in Acts 3 and 4, with her descent in the flying throne, were put in for a revival around 1608–9, a time when he was engaged upon two other plays with similar scenes of aerial thrones in them. These were *Cymbeline* and *Pericles, Prince of Tyre*.

PERICLES, PRINCE OF TYRE: CYMBELINE

Pericles and *Cymbeline* are two romances set in what was, for Shakespeare's audiences, the very glamorous surrounding of classical antiquity. For the Elizabethans, the Romans recalled the noble structures of ancient authority: while the Greeks, with their legendary heroes, were the equivalent of what is for us the Age of Chivalry: Troy was their Camelot, Hector and Achilles their Lancelot and Galahad. Such were the educated tastes of the audiences Shakespeare had in mind when he and the King's Men were promoting their new Blackfriars playhouse. It was a roofed hall on the City side of the river Thames, commodiously seated and designed for the patronage of fashionable people. Plays first presented there could later be taken across to the popular Globe on Bankside with an increased esteem, while the reputation of the Globe suffered nothing at all from its connection with the gentrified Blackfriars. However, the title-page of *Pericles*, first printed in 1609, the year after the King's Men had occupied the Blackfriars, did not refer to that prestigious theatre at all, but advertises the play: 'As it hath been divers and sundry times acted by His Majesty's Servants, at the Globe on the Banck-side'. Learned opinion about the dates of composition and the places of first performance for both *Pericles* and *Cymbeline* wanders uncertainly between Bankside and Blackfriars, and between 1608 and 1610; and in any case both houses were closed by an outbreak of the plague during most of that period. But we may be satisfied for our purpose here that, just as both plays shared a similar character of legendary romanticism, so both theatres shared a similarity of stage equipment, including the availability of flying effects. In *Cymbeline* this is made explicit in a stage-direction: in *Pericles* it is implicit in the context.

Pericles, Prince of Tyre is to my mind the most unusual of all Shakespeare's plays. It was written with collaborators at a time when Shakespeare was most actively committed in his work with the King's Men, their two theatres and his own greatest successes. Certainly much of it was written by him, but not all, and it was omitted by his old companions of the Globe when they were editing the First Folio of his collected works. I think of *Pericles* as having been composed and supervised by him during a busy time, from an idea perhaps conceived (as it was partly written) by others, to show off the widening possibilities of their theatrical art. It is a play unusually full of scenic spectacle and innovation. The use of the ancient poet John Gower as commentator and organiser for the staging of one of his own stories is here much more than a simple introductory Chorus. Time and again he is on stage as a narrator and to set the scene: he tells us to think 'this stage the ship / Upon whose decks the sea-tost Pericles appears': and again later, 'Think this his bark', to which the governor of Mytilene comes out from shore in his barge and is welcomed aboard. (At the Globe it is possible that the Governor and his attendants would have climbed a ladder from the yard onto the deck of the stage.) On three occasions Gower comments upon scenes which are being given on the stage in dumb-show, thus anticipating the 'voice-over' techniques of modern screen-drama, to move the story along. Pericles' adventures at sea are hazardous with storms, in which we must suppose the whole force of the Globe's thunder-and-lightning effects would have been loudly rolled out. In one of these storms Pericles is nearly drowned, so then we have *Enter Pericles wet*. In another he loses his baby daughter and his young wife, though both are restored to him in the end by fortune and by a divine intervention, which is the particular special effect with which we are here concerned. Pericles, aboard his ship at anchor off the coast of Mytilene, has found his long lost daughter at last, but now suddenly he is overcome by the sound of music which none but he (and the audience) can hear: 'Most heavenly music. / It nips me into listing, and thick slumber hangs upon mine eyes: let me rest'. They bring him a pillow for his head, and leave him alone on the stage, overwhelmed with the music. Then, according to *modern* stage-directions: *Diana appears to Pericles in a vision*. She comes to bid him go to her temple in Ephesus where, as he is discover, his lost wife Thaisa is serving as a votaress. But whether in a vision or not, or how in fact the goddess enters the scene, or how or when or where she makes her exit, the original text has nothing to say at all. There are no stage-directions, but only a cryptic statement of the goddess' name, set centrally, on its own, between two lines of type, without explanation, thus:

Diana

Clearly, that cannot ever have been intended as a stage-direction, since it directs nothing at all; but we may surmise that the text could have been set up from a note made at some time in the tiring-house, even perhaps from the prompt-copy itself, where the 'Diana' had been written in as a cue for the backstage staff, meaning: 'Here we are to do all the Diana business, as rehearsed'. If that interpretation is correct, we may then suppose that the Diana business would have been done very much as the Hecate business in *Macbeth* had been, only a few months before. The goddess would have descended in a 'creaking throne' from The Heavens, the creaking (if any) covered up by the 'most heavenly music' that is emphasised in the text. (In *Macbeth* it would have been covered by thunder).

45 *Pericles, Prince of Tyre*, 5.1. The vision of Diana. (Conjectured as performed at the Globe.)

The general effect of all this is shown in my drawing on p. 130, as Diana begins her return ascent into Heaven, with Pericles exclaiming 'Celestial Dian, goddess argentine, I will obey thee'. (In this case I suppose Diana would not have descended fully to the stage, but would have spoken from her throne, midway in the air. Hecate, in *Macbeth*, seems to have come right down onto the stage, since she has to return to her 'foggy cloud', which is waiting for her). In my drawing the cloud-piece projecting downwards from the trap, above Diana, is a sophisticated, and perhaps needless, invention of my own. I have supposed that it might be better if, when the trap opens, one does not at first see the lower part of Diana's cloud, and her legs, but only a cloud which descends while the goddess then emerges downwards from behind it. The clouds themselves in this drawing are suggested in English scenic practice by the designs of Inigo Jones for court masques, devised by Ben Jonson and others – admittedly of a later date, but that would affect more the elegance of the design and the technique of scene-painting than the fact of the clouds themselves, which in the earlier public theatre might have been less refined in execution.

Among the collection of Inigo Jones' designs for Jacobean and Caroline court masques, preserved at Chatsworth House, is a drawing of Jupiter descending from Heaven upon an eagle's back, brandishing thunderbolts. Though this is dated for 1632 it may here bring us directly back to 1609 and Shakespeare's *Cymbeline*, believed his first play written for the new Blackfriars theatre. In this long Romano-British romance, in 5.4, the Roman hero Posthumus is cast into prison, where, in his sleep, he sees a vision of the ghosts of his Roman parents and his brothers who implore Jupiter to give his aid in smoothing the complex difficulties of Posthumus and his British wife Imogen. The vision is composed as a masque with poetic speech and solemn music, for at its climax the marble floor of Heaven opens and *Jupiter descends in Thunder and Lightning, sitting upon an Eagle: he throws a Thunder-bolt. The ghosts fall on their knees.* The god then speaks, promising his help and blessing for the good fortune of the Romano-British wedding, concluding with 'Mount, Eagle to my Palace Christaline', and he *Ascends.* The ascent is covered by eight lines of verse, and takes one minute to perform before one of the ghosts announces: 'The marble pavement closes, he is entered his radiant roof.' With this, and two more concluding lines, they all *Vanish*, and Posthumus awakes. It may be noted here that whereas at the Globe the Heavens ceiling was, or is from good evidence thought to have been decorated with clouds, or a starry zodiac, as is shown in the illustration on p. 130, The Heavens at the Blackfriars (and perhaps other parts of the stage also) seem to have been painted to resemble marble.

THE TEMPEST

A tempestuous noise of Thunder and Lightning heard. Such is the stage direction that opens this, the first play in the first published collection of Shakespeare's works; and it is a Special Effect. At the Globe – if we may assume that *The Tempest* was in fact presented there, though it is not certain – that 'tempestuous noise' would have been one of the most arresting special effects in the repertory, certainly as impressive in a Jacobean public theatre of 1611 – possibly even more so – as anything that can be done with recorded sound in a modern theatre. As noted earlier, that sound, in Jacobean times, was made by rolling iron cannon balls in long wooden troughs across a wooden floor, which at the Globe would have been the floor above the painted Heavens, directly over the stage and above the heads of all the audience gathered around. It must have been a very awe-inspiring sound. The method was taken up as common practice in later theatres; but on those stages the introduction of painted scenery displaced it to other positions behind or at the sides of the scenic arrangements where it could not have had quite the same effectiveness as it had had with the overhead crash and rumble in the original public theatre Heavens.

Even so, Ben Jonson was not satisfied. In the same verse of his Prologue to *Every Man In His Humour* wherein he deplored the descent of the 'creaking throne' he went on to disparage also the 'nimble squib' (of stage lightning) seen 'to make afeard the gentlewomen'. Nor, he continued, is 'roll'd bullet heard / To say, it thunders; nor tempestuous drum / Rumbles to tell you when the storm doth come. . . .' In fact for this occasion Jonson was writing not for the open Globe playhouse, but for the Blackfriars, where the 'rolled bullet' being presumably not quite so effective as I have tried to describe it at the Globe, was augmented with a drum. At this indoor theatre, however, the tricks for producing lightning could have had a better advantage. Even the 'nimble squib' (possibly rocketed down on a wire) could have been taken for a passable thunderbolt, while the device of blowing powdered resin through a candle-flame (shown in the diagram on p. 125) would, I guess – for I have not seen it tried – have created a very fine flash, in the more subdued light-level of the candle-lit Blackfriars.

Excellent though it might have been to have heard that opening 'tempestuous noise' rumbling across the Heavens at the Globe, nothing in *The Tempest* thereafter has the character of a presentation in the older style of the public playhouses. During the first decade of King James' reign in England, and with the direct encouragement of his royal patronage, the newly appointed King's Men turned their attention towards the tastes of the Jacobean court and its courtiers in the more exclusive conditions of their newly adopted 'private' Blackfriars theatre, an indoor playhouse for which, as Professor Gurr has argued,[3] the play of *The Tempest* was specifically written.

The Blackfriars was a conversion built into an upper part of the old Dominican (Black Friars) priory after it had been taken over for lay uses, following the Dissolution of the Monasteries in Henry VIII's time. The theatre there had first been made for the use of choir-boy actors in 1576 (coincidentally the same year the first public playhouse, the old Theatre, was erected in Shoreditch by James Burbage) and it continued in the occupation of boy-players' companies, rivalling the men's companies with some success until the end of the century, when the Burbages acquired the lease of it. They did not make full use of it, however, until 1608, when the King's Men finally set themselves up there, running it permanently in conjunction with the Globe across the river. The long, pitched roof of the western range of the old priory buildings may be seen as still in existence when the topographical artist W. Hollar drew it in the middle 1630s for his remarkable *Long View of London*. The Blackfriars theatre probably occupied the upper part of the riverward end of that long building, under that roof. According

3 *Shakespeare Survey* 41.

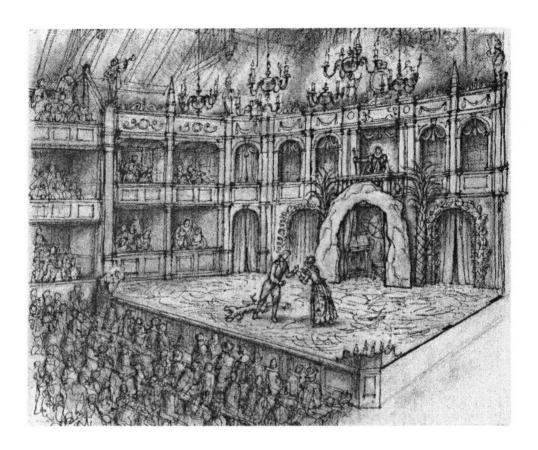

46 *The Tempest*, 3.1. (As at Blackfriar's Theatre.) Prospero's 'cell',
with Ferdinand and Miranda, and Prospero 'on the top'.

to the architect and scholar Irwin Smith[4] the span of the interior, beneath that roof, was forty-six feet. In that case, allowing for ramps of seating with a gallery above, around the 'pit' of the seated auditorium, passageways behind for access to these and the stage boxes on other divisions, we would have a stage with a width of about twenty-three feet, which I show approximately in my sketch on p. 134. As a reconstruction of the general appearance of the Blackfriars it is of course conjectural. (If it were drawn again I think it should be amended by putting aisles for access down the sides and centre of the auditorium).

The drawing shows the stage as specially decorated for *The Tempest*; that is, the painted rocky opening, as for a cave, has been added to decorate the front of the permanent discovery space, here with its curtains drawn back to show the setting of Prospero's 'cell', with his magic book, and a background suitably painted with magical emblems. The rocky cave-mouth which stands in front of this is a piece of painted scenery, similar to Inigo Jones' designs for the scenery in Ben Jonson's *Mask of Oberon*, which was presented at King James' court in 1611 – the same season, as it happens, that Shakespeare's *Tempest* was also given there. Here in this picture of its presentation at the Blackfriars, the entrances to the stage on each side of the 'cave' are garlanded with fresh greenery to help give an Arcadian effect for Prospero's island, and the stage is strewn with fresh rushes. The exotic detail of two palm trees may be thought an unlikely observation for this date, but I find an Italian engraving showing scenery for a masque, with painted palm trees in it, of a date before 1611, and similar prints from the engraver, Giulio Parigi, had found their way to England at that time.

The action on the stage shows Ferdinand and Miranda, in 3.1, wherein they reveal their love for each other. They are observed by Prospero from a distance, though in the text it does not indicate where or how, merely that the lovers are unaware of him. I have therefore taken my cue from a similar situation in a scene further on where he is secretly watching an action on the stage with the direction '. . . *Prosper on the top (invisible)*'. So he is certainly 'above'; but 'on the top' of what? I have assumed he must have been on the

4 Irwin Smith, *Shakespeare's Blackfriars Playhouse* (New York University Press, 1964).

upper stage, and 'on the top' of that small central porch projecting from it, a feature which may be seen in other of my reconstructions herein.[5]

Now having once moved themselves indoors, away from the popular surrounding of their 'wooden O' playhouse into the more exclusive and intimate, though still crowded, rectangle of a theatre in a specially adapted hall, the nature of playgoing and play-showing began to change. The way, in fact, was open for the playhouses of the long frontal view and the scenic perspective, though this was not developed for ordinary public theatres for another fifty years. But the nature of theatrical 'special effects' began to change. The grand processions around the stage, the long descent of the gods from the high Heavens and the devils with their fireworks scrambling noisily out of Hell could not be so effective among the seated patrons indoors. More ingenious tricks, to be seen at closer range, now needed to be invented. *The Tempest* itself is a product of the more sensitive, intimate 'indoor' style. The delicate Ariel was better seen and heard at the closed Blackfriars than at the open Globe. So must have been the tantalising banquet in 3.3, with Prospero 'on the top'. That stage-direction, quoted above, reads in full as follows:

> *Solemn and strange Music: and Prosper on the top (invisible:) Enter several strange shapes, bringin in a Banket; and dance about it with gentle actions and salutations, and inviting the King, etc. to eat, they depart.*

I show my idea of the Banquet and the Strange Shapes in fig. 47. It may be necessary to remind ourselves that a 'banquet' in Jacobean times was not in itself a great feast, but a social preliminary to one, with drinks and delicacies served from a small table, as is seen in the drawing. This 'Banket' on its smaller table is of course easier for the Strange Shapes to carry onto the stage, and it also allows for the better execution of another Special Effect. Prospero's noble but treacherous enemies, being now shipwrecked on his island, are tempted towards the luxurious table to refresh themselves: but on the instant: – *Thunder and Lightning. Enter Ariel (like a Harpy) claps his wings upon the table, and with a quaint device the Banquet vanishes.* My

---

5 It is a feature of my own invention, but one so simple, so obvious and so useful in so many cases that if I could be shown any reason why the Elizabethans never used such a thing, I should find it very hard to believe.

"... Enter several strange shapes
bringing in a banquet ..."

"... and with a quaint
device the banquet
vanishes."

47 *The Tempest, 3.3. Enter several strange shapes bringing in a banquet;* and *Enter Ariel (like a Harpy) claps his wings upon the table, and with a quaint device the banquet vanishes.* (Quaint device here conjectural.)

drawing attempts to show what that 'quaint device' might have been. We see Ariel dressed as the avenging harpy, with his wings which must not be so large he cannot easily manage them, while still being large enough to cover and hide the table top. At the same time (with his foot?) he trips the catch which turns the whole table top and its fixed-on banquet over and upside down, all with one sweep of his wings.

THE THIRD PART OF HENRY VI

We conclude this chapter with an interpretation of one other 'device', this one not 'quaint', like the magical banquet in *The Tempest*, but intended as very spectacular. It is presented in Act 2 of the last play of the *Henry VI* trilogy, and it is taken directly from Holinshed's Chronicle, wherein Edward Prince of Wales and Richard of Gloucester are marching with their army

> in a fair plain near to Mortimer's Cross, not far from Hereford east. . . . At which time (as some write) the sun appeared like three suns, and suddenly joined altogether into one. Upon which sight [Prince Edward] took such courage that he fiercely setting upon his enemies, put them to flight; and for this cause men imagined . . . he gave the sun in his full brilliance for his badge or cognizance.

So in Act 2 of the play we have the entry of Prince Edward and Richard of Gloucester 'and their power', and they are brought to a halt upon the stage, startled by this vision in the sky. 'Dazzle mine eyes, or do I see three suns?' exclaims Edward. 'Three glorious suns', replies Richard, 'each one a perfect sun. . . . See, see, they join, embrace and seem to kiss... Now they are but one lamp, one light, one sun. . . .' It must be understood from the Folio text that this vision was not merely something performed by the actors as though it were a delusion; and indeed a stage-direction, not given in the Folio, is provided in the Quarto version, where *Three suns appear in the air.* Clearly this was, in its day, a mechanical Special Effect of a very striking nature, specially and elaborately made for this one play. I have attempted to reconstruct it in my drawing on p. 139. In doing so I have needed to show the rods and pulleys of its working parts more clearly than need have been seen in reality. Allowing for this, and with the suns themselves brightly polished or painted, I think it would have worked surprisingly well.

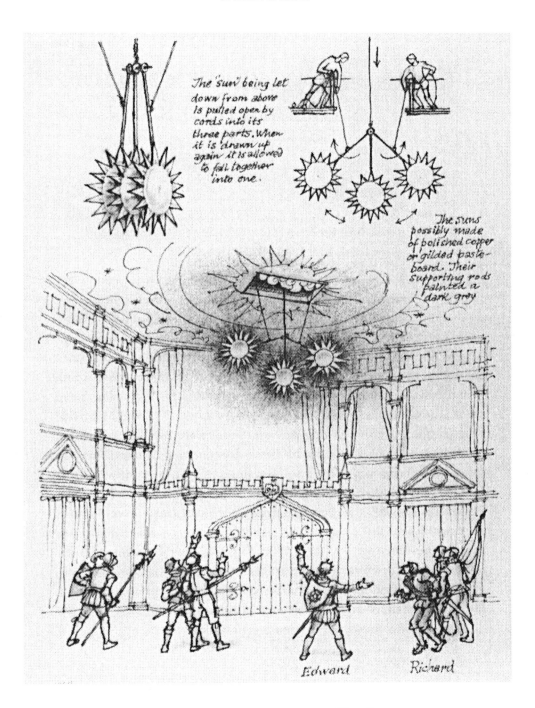

The 'sun' being let down from above is pulled open by cords into its three parts. When it is drawn up again it is allowed to fall together into one.

The suns possibly made of polished copper or gilded pasteboard. Their supporting rods painted a dark grey

Edward   Richard

48 *The Third Part of King Henry VI.* The Three Suns.

CHAPTER NINE

PLAYING AWAY: PRESENTATION IN GREAT HALLS

·

TWELFTH NIGHT; THE COMEDY OF ERRORS; LOVE'S LABOUR'S LOST

Although they were now well-established in their permanent London theatres, the player companies did not altogether lose touch with their earlier mode of life, of travelling the roads between provincial cities and noblemen's great houses in the country. Indeed they could hardly afford not to do so. Whenever London was stricken by outbreaks of the plague, as happened increasingly, sometimes with great severity, towards the end of the sixteenth century, all the London theatres were at once closed down by law, as being obviously dangerous breeding places for the contagion.[1] It should be noted that, for this, a basic problem would be the need for the continual adaptation of plays which had been written for the settled conditions and equipment of the regular playhouses, to allow for the various hazards of acting places that did not offer such facilities. So at those times the players packed up their gear and took to the roads again. Meanwhile at any normal time in London they might be called upon to take one of their plays across the river for presentation in the royal palace of Whitehall, or one of the noblemen's great houses along the Strand, or at the Inns of Court. These last were the collegiate societies of lawyers which trained young gentlemen not only in the law, but in all the refined accomplishments a gentleman was supposed to have, dancing, singing, music and literature. The young lawyers of the Inns of

---

1 In 1592 the theatres were closed, and remained so for two years, during an outbreak which caused 11,000 deaths. They were closed again in 1603 for another year, with a record of 30,000 deaths. Between these two dates there were other occasional visitations, though less severe.

Court as a body represented the development of an intellectual middle-class, and they were boisterously enthusiastic patrons of the theatres.

There were four Inns of Court in Shakespeare's day: Lincoln's Inn, Gray's Inn, and the Inns of the Middle and Inner Temple, and each had its own Great Hall where they dined communally, and entertained. Two of these grand buildings survive and may be seen today just as they were when Shakespeare knew them, and in each of these it is on record that one of his plays was performed. They are Middle Temple Hall, where the players performed *Twelfth Night*, and Gray's Inn where they acted *The Comedy of Errors*. But although in these buildings, by contrast to the theatres which have all disappeared, we may still see the actual backgrounds against which these plays were set up in Shakespeare's own time – even, possibly, under his own direction – the question still remains for us: just how, or in what part of the hall were they performed? I have attempted with my drawings here to imagine some answers.

TWELFTH NIGHT (MIDDLE TEMPLE HALL)

Two dates are advanced for the earliest performances of this play, and both are 'private' stagings in great halls. The earlier date is that proposed by Leslie Hotson[2] who finds reason to believe it was acted for Queen Elizabeth at court on the night of 6 January (i.e., Twelfth Night) in 1601. The other is given by one John Manningham, himself a lawyer, who actually witnessed a performance and entered it in his diary for 2 February 1602. It was then given in the hall of the Middle Temple, of which he was a collegiate member. It is this performance that I attempt to show on my drawing on p. 142. I imagine it here being acted against the background of its famous Hall Screen, then only about thirty years old. (By chance, that makes it broadly contemporary with the building of the earliest public playhouses).

The original function of hall screens was to shield the body of the hall from the draught of the outer entrances, and from the kitchens and other services beyond. Their traditional form provided two wide entrances with a gallery above, which was sometimes – as at the Middle Temple – fronted along with an open range of windows. This form of screen frontage has reminded

2 Leslie Hotson, *The First Night of Twelfth Night*, 1954.

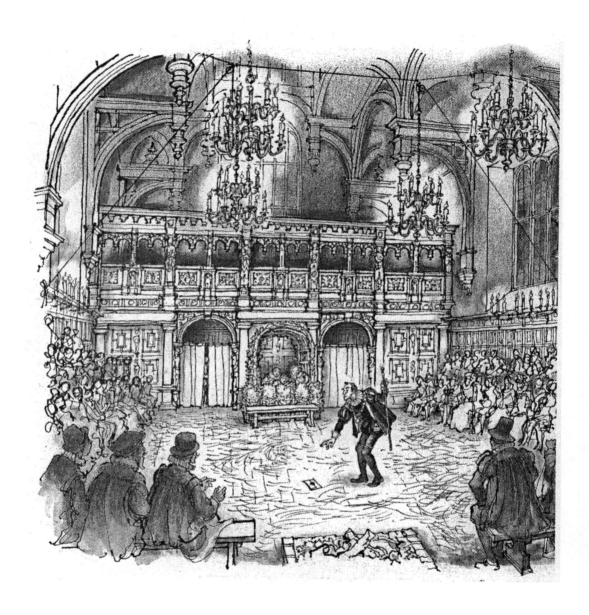

49 *Twelfth Night*, 2.5. As performed in Middle Temple Hall in February 1602.

Elizabethan theatre scholars[3] of the facades of the original public playhouses, as shown in the drawing of the Swan theatre p. 14; but there, at least superficially, the resemblance ends, for the eye looking upwards into the vault of the roof finds nothing to suggest any possible way of putting in a Heavens there with an apparatus for flying. Reconstructors who wish to take the hall screen as a basis for an Elizabethan tiring-house frontage and wish at the same time, as some do, to abolish the idea of a 'discovery space' opening, are therefore quick to point out that at the Middle Temple there is no sign, nor indeed very much room between the doors for any such central opening, thus finding support for a theory that there never was such a thing. (Nevertheless if there were not, the lack of it would often have to be supplied by other means).

The scene in my picture is of course quickly recognised: Malvolio finding the letter dropped in his path to entrap his vanity. But there has also to be a place for three other people – Sir Toby, Andrew Aguecheek and Fabian – to spy on him from hiding, being themselves part of the action, seen and heard by everyone in the hall except, of course, Malvolio. The hiding place itself is described in the dialogue as a 'box-tree', and a usual modern device is to make a topiary box-hedge of it, with the three watchers bobbing up and down to speak from behind it. Therefore I have placed a hedge forward of the space between the doors, and have put a convenient bench in front of it, upon which Malvolio might sit to read his letter, thus effectively concentrating all the comic business together in one place. There are of course alternatives. An obvious one would be to place the hedge actually in one of the two door openings; but this arrangement would in effect draw the action back behind the screen instead of allowing it to come forward into the body of the hall, which is certainly the better way. But there is a scene further on (4.2) where the opposite may be done: Malvolio's 'prison' where, as a supposed madman, he is laid 'in hideous darkness' and is visited by the Clown in the guise of the curate 'Sir Topas'. The Clown speaks from outside, to (stage direction) *Malvolio within*. One may therefore suppose that Malvolio's voice is heard from behind a curtain hung across the doorway, for the whole first part of their dialogue is concerned with the darkness of Malvolio's confinement –

3 Cf. Richard Hosley, 'The Origins of the Shakespearean Playhouse', *Shakespeare Quarterly* (Spring 1964).

not only 'hideous' but 'dark as hell', 'dark as ignorance', and 'remain thou still in darkness', etc. I say we 'may suppose' a curtain and the voice from behind it, but there is another possibility, that upon a playhouse stage, instead of the solid floor of a hall, Malvolio's hellish prison might have been located in the traditional 'Hell' beneath the stage, with Sir Topas speaking to him down a trap. Possible though that is, I think as a dialogue it would have been less audible, and so the curtain method would still have been better. However, as the scene goes on both suppositions become harder to sustain. In print the dialogue is of nearly one hundred lines, covering two and a half pages. I cannot think that for all that time Malvolio was obliged to act unseen behind a curtain and within the wall of the screen. Possibly the curtain would have drawn back so that Malvolio could actually be seen 'within' at least by a part of the audience (for not all could get a view within the door): or possibly a door could have been devised for him to come out onto the stage with him, and he and the Clown to hold their dialogue, one on each side of it: we will return to this possibility in the next section, with a similar circumstance in *The Comedy of Errors*. Meanwhile it is likely that the 'box hedge' from the earlier scene, which in the smaller of my two drawings on pp. 142–3 I show as being still in position during the 'duel' scene in 3.4, would have had to be taken away at the end of Act 2, to clear the acting area and the lines of sight at that point.

We should now briefly take note of two features which were a standing accompaniment of play presentation in all great halls, and may be seen in this picture of the Middle Temple, as well as the one of Gray's Inn, which is to follow. These are the chandeliers and the hearth. We may presume that while a dinner was being served much of the light in the hall would be given by candles placed along the tables, but for the entertainment afterwards the entire space of the hall must be cleared and the chandeliers all lit and hauled up to give more light. We find all this in *Romeo and Juliet*, 1.4, with old Capulet busying about with preparations for the ball after supper:

> A hall, a hall, give room . . .
> More light you knaves, and turn the tables up:
> And quench the fire, the room is grown too hot.

With all the chandeliers alight, the roof timbers and plastering of these great halls must have been very much darkened with candle smoke by the end of the winter. (In later times, after the ceiling of Inigo Jones' Banqueting House in Whitehall had been decorated with the paintings of Peter Paul Rubens, that hall was never again used for entertainments by candlelight, and thus the paintings are still there to be seen in good condition today.) The hearth, however, was a different matter, and thus I show it in my picture, but, as instructed by old Capulet, with its fire now quenched. I have placed them correctly, not in the centre of the hall but further towards the dais end of it, thus leaving a greater clearance of floor space in front of the screen. The original positions, like this, of the fireplaces at both Middle Temple and Gray's Inn halls may be ascertained by the smoke-louvres which were placed directly overhead, above the hearths, and are still to be seen in the high vaults of their roofs.

This greater floor-space in front of the screen, making it more suitable for the presentation of plays, together with the screen's own resemblance to the tiring-house frontage in a public theatre, would seem to confirm that the screen end of the hall, rather than the dais end, was the natural and proper location for plays given in halls of this type; and indeed that must surely have been usual. But before finally settling for this arrangement we find ourselves confronted by a contradiction. The most extensive contemporary account of entertainments given in a hall (and which in this case included a play by Shakespeare) describes it in terms that seem to show they were not given against the background of the screen, but the other way round, at the dais end. The hall in this case is the one at Gray's Inn.

THE COMEDY OF ERRORS (GRAY'S INN HALL)

It was customary at the illustrious and wealthy Inns of Court to celebrate Christmas and the New Year with a season of Revels that lasted, on and off, until the beginning of Lent. The Revels at Gray's Inn over the midwinter of 1594–5 were to be especially notable because for the two previous winters they had had to be cancelled owing to continuing outbreaks of the plague, and so the Master Benchers and students of the Inn were now eager to restore their Revels, which were highly reputed; but they are notable also because on this occasion an anonymous member had decided to keep a record of it all. He wrote it in heroic terms with the Latin title *Gesta*

Grayorum, which might be translated in suitably mock-heroic terms as *The Doughty Deeds of the Grayites*, and it had a subtitle in English: *The History of the High and Mighty Prince Henry, Prince of Purpoole . . . who reigned and died AD 1594*: 'Purpoole' was a corruption of the name Portpoole, the City parish in which Gray's Inn was situated, and 'Prince Henry' was a certain Henry Helmes of Norfolk, a prominent member of the Inn who had been elected as a traditional 'Lord of Misrule', to preside over that year's festivities. The 'Grayites' took these matters seriously enough, and in the *Gesta Grayorum* Henry Helmes is consistently referred to as 'The Prince' or 'His Highness'.

Matters, however, did not on this occasion go so smoothly as had been hoped. On the evening of Holy Innocents' Day (28 December), when a particularly grand celebration had been planned, the general anticipation of it caused such crowds to gather in the hall that it became impossible to keep order, and when the night's special guests arrived, an 'Ambassador' from the Inner Temple, 'very gallantly appointed, and attended by a great number of brave Gentlemen', the crush within the hall developed from disorder into 'tumult'. A stage had been built in the hall not only for the presentation of the shows but for the honourable seating of special guests, but 'there arose such a disordered Tumult and Crowd upon the Stage that there was no opportunity to effect that which was intended'. The Ambassador from the Inner Temple and his 'Templarians' eventually gave it all up and departed, with evident displeasure. But the 'throngs and Tumults' continued, so that the planned entertainments, which had been devised 'especially for the gracing of the Templarians', had to be abandoned. 'It was thought good not to offer anything of Account, saving Dancing and Revelling with Gentlewomen; and after such Sports, a Comedy of Errors . . . was played by the players. So that Night was begun and continued to the end, in nothing but Confusion and Errors'.[4]

It should be noted that 'the players' referred to above could have been none other than the Chamberlain's Men, and it is remarkable that they were so ready and able to fill in with a comedy like this, as a stop-gap and at such short notice. They had been the previous night acting before the Queen and her court at Greenwich Palace, twelve miles away down the river, and

4 Quoted from 'Shakespeare and the Prince of Purpoole' by Margaret Knapp and Michal Kobialka, in *Theatre History Studies*, vol. 4, 1984.

perhaps it had been the Errors play they had presented there, so that they could have had it all ready with them. However that may have been, they certainly saved a difficult situation for the Gentlemen of Gray's Inn. On the next evening those same gentlemen, in the course of their Revels, directed that an enquiry at law should be made into the causes of those 'great Disorders and Abuses lately done', which they suspected were due to sorcery and witchcraft, from which they had had to be rescued by 'a Company of base and common Fellows . . . with a Play of Errors and Confusions'. Meanwhile, for our purposes here the illustration shows the play being given, not as in fact it was in the midst of 'Throngs and Tumults', but as it should or might have been under more orderly conditions.

It is stated in the *Gesta* that a stage had been built in the hall to serve all the various performances during the whole season of Revels, besides being big enough to take all the distinguished guests and 'worshipful Personages' who were to be seated upon it. It is evident the stage would have had to be fairly broad and wide, so the question is, where was it placed? It could not have been against or near the screen, which takes up all the width of the hall at the east end, a distance of about thirty-five feet, and the width of the space there between the two screen doors[5] is not great enough to give room for any useful width of stage; or if the stage were made wider it would obstruct access into the hall. Therefore I have placed the stage at the dais end of the hall, building it all over the dais itself (which would normally be only about six or eight inches high) to a total height of about three feet above the floor. By putting a short flight of steps from the floor up to the stage I have thus combined the functions of the dais, for the elevated seating of honourable

5 It should be noted that the doors of the Gray's Inn screen do not have quite so much height or headroom as those of the Middle Temple, seen in the illustration for *Twelfth Night* p. 142–3. Nevertheless it is stated in the *Gesta Grayorum* that at the enthronement of the Prince of Purpoole at Christmas 1594 there entered into the Great Hall 'the Prince's Champion, all in compleat armour, on horseback, and so came riding about the fire; and in the midst of the hall stayed and made his challenge' (i.e., the formality against any question of the Prince's title). It may be questionable, however, whether the doors were spacious enough to admit such a spectacular visitor upright on horseback with his lance and the plumes of his helmet, even with bending his head. Professor Dorsch, in his edition of the play, has suggested, with a question mark, that this may have been a hobby-horse in a Christmas charade. I think, rather reluctantly, that he may be right.

50 *The Comedy of Errors*, 3.1. As at Gray's Inn Hall, Christmas 1594. (Antipholus of Ephesus shut out of his house door.) The 'Prince of Purpoole' (Master of the Revels) enthroned on the right.

persons, with that of the stage for the acting of plays. This is not without precedent. Queen Elizabeth had once sat in her 'state' upon a stage which had been built for her to see a play in King's College Chapel, Cambridge. That stage had been set across the whole width of the Chapel, and the Queen's throne was placed, under its canopy and backed by its embroidered cloth of State at one end of it, against the Chapel wall. It was essential that royalty attending a play should be as much in view of the audience as the play itself; so here in my illustration on p. 149 we may see His Highness the Prince of Purpoole seated in state on the stage at Gray's Inn for a performance of *The Comedy of Errors*. The Prince is attended by all his train and by 'Lords, Ladies and worshipful Personages', but, as stated above, I have much reduced the numbers of these to make better space for the play and to allow entrance for the actors from openings in the curtains at the back, where in the public theatres the tiring house doors would be. As for the comedy itself, this has been carefully composed out of a knitting of confusions based upon two pairs of identical twins who can be distinguished chiefly, I suppose, by some difference of colouring in their otherwise identical costumes. What I show here is Scene 1 of Act 3, where the whole thing turns itself almost literally inside out, showing the inside and outside of a house in which all parties are claiming the right to be on either side of the door. Though this may be staged in any number of fanciful ways, in fact the only article of scenery that is really needed for this scene is the door itself. It should be remembered that the Chamberlain's Men had mounted this play at Gray's Inn at very short notice. With no time at all to make special arrangements, I suggest they simply brought themselves and their costumes with one property door across from Bankside to Gray's Inn, and with only the clearing of some space on the stage everything was thus ready for them. For this scene, on cue, two of their tiremen carried in and held the door as needed. I show the tiremen with hoods over their heads as a sort of indication that they are supposed to be invisible.

LOVE'S LABOUR'S LOST

This comedy was first published in 1598, though it is believed to have been written some years earlier for a company of boy players. It would certainly

PLAYING AWAY: PRESENTATION IN GREAT HALLS

have been suitable for such. In a *dramatis personae* of eighteen parts, at least ten, including five for 'women', could properly have been played by boys, and the rest more or less easily adapted. Professor Alfred Harbage in an Introduction to the play[6] has said: 'It is conceivable that Shakespeare wrote the play for [The Children of] Paul's theatre in 1588–89 and salvaged it as a novelty for his own company in 1596–97'. I will take advantage of a certain liberty Harbage seems to allow in the dating, to steal another year or two for my own purpose, which is to surmise a possible presentation of *Love's Labour's Lost* in 1594–5, thus bringing it within touching distance of *The Comedy of Errors* at Gray's Inn, from which we have just taken leave. My reason is that I am intrigued here by something that might be called 'the Russian connection'.

It will be remembered that the season of Christmas Revels at Gray's was presided over by one Henry Helmes, with the revelry title of Prince of Purpoole. The Revels continued in fact for six weeks, but it is recorded in the *Gesta Grayorum*, that at a Twelfth Night banquet given by the Prince there entered an Ambassador from the Emperor of Russia asking the Prince's help (in some matter not disclosed), which the Prince promptly agreed to give, offering to bring an army with him into the bargain. Thereupon, the next day the Prince set out for Russia with the Ambassador. Three weeks later, his mission accomplished, the Prince was back again, and sent orders ahead of him for the officers of his court to meet him the next day at Blackwall, six miles down river from London Bridge, which of course they did; and so the Prince of Purpoole returned in state to London, with an escort of fifteen barges, with trumpets and music and flags flying, and the firing of cannons in salute. They pulled in at Greenwich on the way, so that the Prince could send in his compliments to the Queen at her palace there, and then proceeded to the Tower where the Prince disembarked and rode in procession with a hundred horsemen through the streets to Gray's Inn and another fine banquet.

But what, in real terms, could all this mean? It is obviously fanciful. Henry Helmes, whether Prince of Purpoole or not, could not possibly have travelled to Russia and back by sailing ship, even by the shortest sea route via

6 In *The Pelican Shakespeare: The Complete Works* (London, Allen Lane, The Penguin Press, 1969).

the Baltic to the Russian port of Narva, in the depths of winter, and back again all fit and fine and ready for dinner, in just three weeks, leaving aside the execution of whatever the business was he went for. We must therefore guess that Helmes, a distinguished and busy lawyer of Gray's Inn, may have had some business in hand with the Russian trade, perhaps through the Muscovy Company (which still exists, and had been established in London since 1553). It is possible to imagine that that Company either had or used a wharf at Blackwall, and that there was business with shipping and excise there, with which Helmes had to be concerned. This could have been the 'Russia' he went to with the 'Ambassador' for three weeks, before he was back again in his Purpoole principality for the last few days of the Revels. There we may now leave him, and return again to our business with *Love's Labours Lost*, where we find reason to think that Shakespeare, and his audiences also in the early 1590s, were intrigued by their early contacts with that vast, scarcely known Christian empire on the far side of distant Poland. Among the great sea-captains of the Elizabethan age, of the generation of Drake and Hawkins and the Spanish Main, we should also remember Richard Chancellor who sailed northwards around to the ports of Narva and Archangel, and travelled to Moscow and the court of Ivan the Terrible. Russia was a country every whit as exotic as Mexico and the remote Bermudas. It is in this context that we should understand the entry of the maskers in 5.2, of *Love's Labour's Lost*, which is shown here on pp.154–5.

In this drawing I have supposed that the play is being performed privately in the great hall of a nobleman's house for an audience of his household friends and guests. (Rather faintly in the background I show him in conversation with the playwright, who stands beside him). The action shown here is towards the end of the play where everything is put into a pleasant confusion of masking and mistaken identities, in a scene of romantic elegance. The Princess of France and her ladies have exchanged among themselves the 'favours' sent them by their courtly lovers, the King of Navarre and his friends, which they are supposed to wear. But now the Princess has exchanged the rich jewel sent to her, with that of her lady Katherine, for Katherine's jewelled glove, and each is wearing the others' on her sleeve, (as, for the keen-sighted, I have shown). Then a trumpet sounds, and the Princess's chamberlain Boyet announces the arrival of the noble courtiers in a masque. The stage direction reads: *Enter Black moores with musicke, the Boy with a speech, and the rest of the Lords disguised*. They are in fact disguised as Muscovites – or 'a mess of Russians', as the Princess laughingly describes them, later. But this brings in a consideration I had not foreseen when I made this drawing. The picture purports to be a 'reconstruction' of an early performance of this play; but in such a case how can we know or show what costumes the original actors in it had to wear? For instance, it has been disclosed to the Princess and her ladies on the stage – and so to us in the audience – that Navarre and his companions are about to enter disguised as 'Russians', and we in our time, well-educated in a world full of informative pictures, will surely have at least a superficial knowledge, if no more, of a supposedly 'Russian' appearance; but at the same time we may ask ourselves, what was an Elizabethan wardrobe mistress in the tiring-house supposed to find or prepare for this purpose, what if anything did the audience expect to see, and, right or wrong, how or what was anyone to know, whatever the result? In making my reconstruction here I may seek the help of books on costume history, with ample references for rich and fashionable dress of the first Queen Elizabeth's time; and if I find rather less to help me with my Russians, I feel I am free, if necessary, to make something up, based upon whatever I have found, and supplemented from my own imagination, which it happens I have preferred to do in this case. Thus my Russians here are something I might have designed as a modern production-designer of the play, and not as the Elizabethans might have conceived them, which in fact we do not know, except for a hint in one line towards the end of the scene (5.2), where one of the Princess's ladies describes the appearance of their recently departed visitors. They were, she says, 'Disguised like Muscovites, in shapeless gear.' How are we to understand that word 'shapeless'? Elizabethan fashionable dress for both sexes was, we know, very strongly shaped – buttoned, pointed, padded, puffed and belted – in. Does this mean that by contrast the Muscovites were loosely clad, say in wide thick, robes wrapped about them? Or does 'shapeless' here simply mean 'uncouth'? And should I perhaps revise my drawing in the light of this? I have to confess that I prefer to leave my Russians as they are.

51 *Love's Labour's Lost*, 5.2. Conjectured as performed at a nobleman's great hall in *c.* 1593–4.
The masque of Russians. *Enter Black moors with music, the Boy with a speech,
the rest of the Lords disguised.*

52 *Hamlet*, 5.1. Hamlet and Laertes at Ophelia's graveside.

CHAPTER TEN

DRAWING CONCLUSIONS

·

HAMLET; A MIDSUMMER NIGHT'S DREAM; KING LEAR; KING HENRY VIII

Returning from their excursions into the country and the great halls of their noble patrons, as described in the previous chapter, we may suppose that the player companies re-entered their now well-established permanent play-houses in London with some relief and satisfaction. There they could continue to extend their art and reputation as nowhere else in the country, with large audiences drawn from all classes of society, bringing together an educated middle-class with tradesmen and commoners and visitors from the aristocracy, into the circle of one crowded building. With this picture of an expectant audience pressing around the stage, the scene is here set for a brief examination of four more plays, each one with its own particular question of staging.

HAMLET

That this play was written for, and remained attached to, a purpose-built professional stage, therefore presumably of the Globe, must appear from the conditions of 5.1, the cemetery of Yorick's skull and Ophelia's burial. It is a long scene, a full half-hour of stage time, and it is framed so firmly around the stage's central grave-trap that it may be doubted whether this scene – and therefore the play itself – could ever be performed except in a theatre with a professionally equipped stage. (Nevertheless, even as I write this I must recall that in the spring of 1608 a certain Captain William Keeling, commanding an East India Company's ship the *Dragon*, being becalmed off the coast of Sierra Leone, wrote in his journal that he 'had

Hamlet acted aboard me, which I permit to keep my people from idleness and unlawful games, or sleep.' There is a certain picturesque similarity here between this wooden shipboard performance of the play, with the cargo hatches in the deck possibly opened up to serve as the grave, and the wooden surroundings of a playhouse stage). The stage unfolding of the graveyard scene is here shown, as at the Globe, in the three drawings of fig. 52. The scene has been set by with the opening of the grave-trap, presumably by the two gravediggers as they begin their act. Hamlet and Horatio are shown cloaked and hatted, as arriving from their journey. They are concealed behind one of the stage posts while the funeral procession led by the king enters and passes over the stage at the back. Evidently, in the Elizabethan staging, there must have been some noticeable and demeaning lack of the proper funerary ceremonial ('maimed rites' as Hamlet at once perceives them) which would have been noticed by all the original audience, but with a modern production in our less ceremonious times it is hard to know how this perfunctory degradation can be shown, or make its point so as to explain Laertes' grief and anger when, by the original stage-direction, he 'leaps in the grave'. Thereupon Hamlet comes forward to claim a greater passion than Laertes' – but does he then also leap into the grave? The text does not direct him to, though in the space of six lines from Hamlet's revealing himself they are grappling together and Laertes has him by the throat ('I prithee take thy fingers from my throat'). So now an immediate question is, with Laertes leaping into the grave and Hamlet above him, how can Laertes seize him by the throat? Has Hamlet himself also leaped into the grave? There is no stage-direction to say so, though the king calls out 'Pluck them asunder'. In my illustration I have followed the opinion of Professor Philip Edwards, for whose edition of the play it was originally drawn, that rather than have Hamlet and Laertes scuffling impiously within the confines of Ophelia's grave, Laertes has climbed out to run at Hamlet on the open stage. An incidental point that may therefore be deduced from this scene is that because it so firmly located around the open grave-trap in the stage floor, and because when on tour in the provinces the player companies could hardly have expected to find such a facility readily at hand, and because this scene is so essential to it, Shakespeare's *Hamlet* is not itself a play that was ever taken 'on tour'. It belonged exclusively to the great theatrical ambience of the Globe and the Blackfriars in London. Yet at the same time it contains a vivid representation of the working life of an Elizabethan company on tour, with the scene of the arrival of the players at the court of Elsmore, in Act 3, and their ready performance of the scene Hamlet had written for them. It is difficult to be sure how this play-within-a-play might best have been staged at the Globe, so I show it here in two possible versions (p. 160). In the upper of the two sketches I have assumed that the players have adopted the curtained area at the back of the stage, and we see the Poisoner in Hamlet's play making his entrance to the sleeping king, for whom a carpet has been set to represent the Bank of Flowers on which the stage direction says he is to lie.[1] In the lower sketch I have given over the curtained area to make a frame for the royal thrones, so that the reaction of Claudius and Gertrude to Hamlet's incriminating play may be better seen by the audience. Hamlet himself remains in the most dominant position on the stage, as commentator between the theatre audience and the action of his play. The musicians in the gallery above are given a detailed programme, with *Enter Trumpets and Kettle Drums . . . Danish March. Sound a Flourish*, and later *Hoboyes play* for the entry of the elaborate dumb-show which precedes Hamlet's play itself.

Although my drawings show the musicians placed 'above' for this scene, I have here to admit a certain doubt about that. A stage direction in the later Quarto editions, bidding the trumpets and kettle-drums to *Enter* is unusual, and could be taken to mean either that the music was then to begin playing or that the musicians were no longer in the gallery but had entered the main stage, to take up a position in the background for the play's preliminary dumb-show, which would then be accompanied by the hoboyes throughout. The musicians would presumably have provided a trumpet announcement for the opening of the play itself, and remained on stage until its angry interruption and dismissal by Claudius, with his summary departure: 'Give me some light. Away!'

1 But see also the Bank shown in my picture for *A Midsummer Night's Dream*, p. 163.

53 *Hamlet*, 3.2. Hamlet's play (Miching Mallecho) with alternative positionings for Claudius and Gertrude.

A MIDSUMMER NIGHT'S DREAM

My pictures overleaf show a stage specially decorated for this play with greenery and garlands freshly brought in from the neighbourhood of the theatre, which is shown in Hollar's picture to be surrounded by small trees, so there was no lack of material. The question is whether, for only a few performances at a time – and a showing for even a new play was not usually more than a few days – the company servants would have gone to so much trouble. I like to think that they might have done. The greenery would have wilted a little after a day or two, but it could have been refreshed and added to. The stage would have been strewn as usual with rushes, and we may suppose, to support my picture, that the stage in this case has been specially dressed with garlands for the visit of a noble patron. There is no difficulty with the 'flowery bank', a painted cloth spread over cushions, nor should there be any with the costumes. It will be seen that Bottom's ass's head does not cover the actor's whole face, but leaves him free and unmuffled to speak his lines. In this I have followed an Italian engraving showing animal-headed servants attending a masque in Rome in the 1580's,[2] and it is likely that without a conventional device of this sort an actor in an Elizabethan theatre would have had some difficulty in making himself heard. For the costumes of Theseus and Hippolyta I have followed the mode of heroic classicism which was beginning to find its way into the educated imagination through the medium of the Dutch engraving industry and Italian paintings. Modes of visual imagination, however, are not easy to settle within this play. A particular problem lies with the representation of Elizabethan stage fairies. From their names – Cobweb, Moth, Mustard Seed and the rest – it is clear that we are meant to imagine them as very little creatures, and therefore that they should be played by the smallest boys available to the company; but how many such might there be? Professor R. A. Foakes in his very careful study of the play has considered the known practice of the doubling of parts in the Elizabethan companies, and himself cites the American scholar William A. Ringler Jnr, who has apportioned the twenty-two speaking parts of this play

2 Reproduced in Nicoll, *Stuart Masques and the Renaissance Stage*, p. 206

54 *A Midsummer Night's Dream*, 2.2 and 3.1.
The stage shown as possibly dressed and decorated for a special occasion.

Moth

Oberon
Juck
Peaseblossom
Mustard
Seed.

Cobweb
Bottom
Titania

The lovers sleeping

ⓐ

Hermia Lysander
Helena
Demetrius

Hippolyta Theseus
Egeus

Bottom

ⓑ

55 *A Midsummer Night's Dream*, 4.1.

among a supposed standing company of sixteen actors and four boys. I am not happy, myself, with such a small number of fairies for a play in which they are surely intended to create a specially attractive feature of invention. Foakes considers the possibility that the play may have been first presented privately as part of the wedding celebrations in a noble family,[3] and that in such a case it would be 'plausible to suppose that a private patron would provide several boys to swell the company'. To add to this I would hazard another, different conjecture: is it not possible to suppose that there might have been temporary exchanges between companies, or that the famous Chamberlain's Men might not have hired or borrowed one or two extra boy players from among (for example) those of the Children of Paul's or even of the Chapel Royal, by some limited special agreement? I must suppose it is unlikely, though stranger things than that have been known in the world of the imaginative arts.

We are perhaps on firmer ground in trying to imagine how these boys-as-fairies might have been dressed, though I know of no original source in Elizabethan pictures to guide our vision towards theirs in the imagination of fairyland, and I suppose if such a source should ever come to light it might surprise us as much as did the drawing of the Swan theatre in its own day. I think our best approach for the purpose would be through the mind's eye of Inigo Jones and his designs for dresses in the masques at the court of James I, and I have adopted something of this style for the court of Oberon and Titania, with my own contribution that I think the fairies might have had bare feet.

KING LEAR

The two drawings brought together on p. 166 enclose the whole play between its first scene and its last, and when I laid out the page in this way I imagined it with the title *Lear and His Daughters*. In the upper picture, the intemperate old king is dividing his realm between his two elder daughters,

---

3 The marriage of Elizabeth Carey and Thomas Berkeley in February 1596 is cited as a possible occasion. The bride's grandfather, Lord Hunsdon, and her father Sir George Carey, were both in turn patrons of Shakespeare's company.

and disowning his favourite Cordelia: in the lower, as a result of this abrupt abdication of good judgement, they are all three dead. So far so good, and as a whole drawing I am not dissatisfied with it; but now as a presentation of its intended Jacobean staging I think the second drawing (b) lacks an important element of style and ceremony, and though I do not wish to redraw it I will use it here as a figure for revision.

The arrangement as I show it, of Lear now so tragically reunited with his three daughters is surely what was intended, and that the bodies of Goneril and Regan have been carried in on litters is more or less dictated by the quickness with which the operation of bringing them in is written. The stage management of these last pages of the play appears in the text as such a rapid interplay of events and emotions, that its effective presentation might be described as a sort of choreography; and moreover there are many variations of detail in the printed editions, between the Folio version and the two Quartos. Thus the violent deaths, off-stage, of Goneril and Regan are no sooner announced than the Duke of Albany, who has taken over the de facto control of affairs, commands: 'Produce the bodies, be they alive or dead', and at once, in the Folio version *Goneril and Regan's bodies are brought out*, that is forward from the tiring house onto the stage. It is impossible to suppose that they are simply brought on manhandled as bodies: they must be carried in on litters, as I show them, for ease of management if for no other reason: but I think now that what I have drawn is too much of a battle-field affair, a pair of stretchers, the bodies on them each covered with a mere sheet or blanket. What I had not sufficiently realised – while I was busy making an effect of simplicity with the rush-strewn stage – was that with the bringing-in of these bodies the drama has now entered its formal last phase, that is of tragic ceremonial. The two royal sisters have been brought back to set the scene. They should each be covered not with a mere blanket but with a rich ceremonious pall, of black or purple, embroidered and fringed with gold. This, when the bodies are first brought in, will be turned back so that they may be recognised, but later, at Albany's command to 'Cover their faces', the coverings are drawn up fully over their heads. They are set side by side, but with enough room between them for Lear to come in with the body of Cordelia in his arms, for the final scene when he too will die.

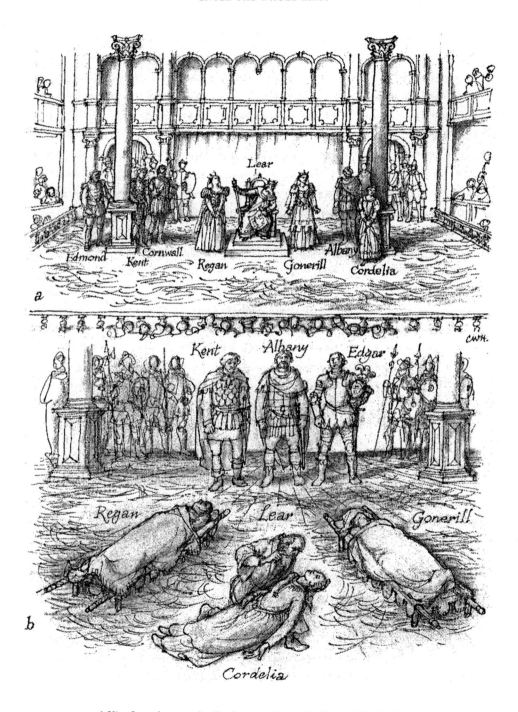

56 *King Lear*, Acts 1 and 5. Beginning and end: the king and his daughters.

The conclusions of the great Jacobean tragedies with their stages formally encumbered with its ritual doom of dead bodies is accepted nowadays as a convention making up with a grand style for what it lacks in pathos. Possibly this was always the case. But whereas in a modern theatre we can make a gentle and convenient closure to such scenes by the descent of a slow curtain or the dimming out of lights, on the open daylight stage of Shakespeare's time there was no other way but to clear the stage by the carrying-out of the bodies. For this reason it must at first seem strange that the bodies of Goneril and Regan, whose deaths offstage have already been announced and described to us, should now be brought on, only to be carried off again so soon after. The purpose can only be for the sake of what, above, I called a tragic ceremonial. For this reason, according to my would-be revision of this picture, the bodies of the two sisters are now covered with their palls of black, purple and gold, making a proper tragic setting for the death of Lear with the dead Cordelia. Then, while the last funerary speeches of the play are spoken by Kent and Edgar into the hushed auditorium, two other litters are quietly brought in at the back, and the old king and Cordelia are laid upon them and covered with their palls. I imagine that Cordelia's will be black like her sisters', but Lear's would be of royal purple. And with this Edgar speaks his valediction: 'The oldest hath borne most. We that are young / Shall never see so much nor live so long.' Then: *Exeunt with a Dead March.*

KING HENRY VIII

Shakespeare's histories were all written in the 1590s, that is during the last years of Queen Elizabeth. If they had been written as a sequence in historical order they might have been supposed as forming a great English national epic – a 'Henriciad' – based upon the Kings Henry IV, V and VI, and ending with the overthrow of the medieval kingdom under Richard III; but there had been no such formal intention, The plays combine into two groups, separated by a gap of three years in the writing, with the later parts of the history preceding the earlier.

Henry VI, which is full of fighting and marching, and drums and colours, was actually staged before the historically earlier *Henry V*, which, despite

The Masters →

King Henry

Wolsey

Anne
Bullen

57 *King Henry VIII*, 1.4. The last play at the first Globe. (The 'idle smoke' of 29 June 1613.)

the name and fame of Agincourt, is concerned not so much with the battle itself, which takes place off stage, but rather with the lives and actions of individuals concerned in it before and after. It is a drama of a different and more humane kind than the earlier histories: after this, Shakespeare wrote no more history plays for twelve years, until in 1613 he presented the King's Men with *The Famous History of King Henry VIII*, which is the last play of the orthodox Shakespeare canon, and was written in collaboration with John Fletcher, the younger poet who on Shakespeare's retirement, succeeded him at the Globe as the company's regular dramatist.

Henry the Eighth was conceived in a very different mode from the earlier histories, which were full of heroic confrontations and warfare. This play by comparison is formal, rhetorical and processional. Its spectacular qualities, however, are emphasised throughout, and its parades are described in stage-directions of unusual detail, as, for example, with *The Order of the Coronation* of Anne Bullen, which names a procession of nineteen great officers of State, with their coronets, robes and staffs of office, coming from Westminster Abbey, with the newly-crowned Queen, who proceeds under a canopy borne by four of the Wardens of the Cinque Ports, *the Queen in her Robe, richly adorned with Pearl, crowned. On each side of her the Bishops of London and Winchester*, and, following her, *the old Duchess of Norfolk, in a Coronall of gold wrought with Flowers, bearing the Queen's Train.* They are followed by other 'Ladies and Countesses, with plain circlets of gold without Flowers'. They *Exeunt, first passing over the stage in Order and State, and then A great Flourish of Trumpets.* It is to be noted that the procession is directed to *pass over* the stage, that is keeping towards the back of it between the two tiring house doors, not to *go about* it, which would bring them forward, where there are now two gentlemen posted to describe it all with a commentary, for the audience's benefit, pointing out the eminent persons as they pass: 'A royal train, believe me: who's that bears the sceptre?' 'The Marquess of Dorset; and that the Earl of Surrey, with the rod', and so on.

At this point we should pause a moment to consider the portrayal on the stage of the play's central figure, the king himself. In our century, with its wealth of photographic reproductions of pictures from even the remotest times, the personal appearance of Henry VIII is for us among the most familiar of all the monarchs of history: but would it have been so for the Jacobeans of Shakespeare's audience? For them the legendary tyrant had been dead for more than sixty years, and although there were people still alive whose fathers might actually have seen him long ago, how many were there who could usefully have been able to describe his appearance to Shakespeare and his actors? Certainly there existed, possibly then at Hampton Court, a famous portrait of him by Hans Holbein, which for us has fixed the image of Henry VIII firmly in the historical imagination; but in Shakespeare's time we cannot be sure that the playwright or his actors had ever seen it. Or even if they had, and if great trouble had been taken to achieve a resemblance to it on the stage, how many among the audiences at the Globe might have known how right or wrong it was? This being so it would presumably have been enough for an actor of commanding presence to adopt certain famous characteristics of the King's personal manner, as handed down by legend and report, which could be brought into his act — such as his loud 'ha!' when he was vexed or impatient, which in fact comes into the play or is commented upon several times.[4]

The alternative title for this play is *All Is True*, and we may suppose that no effort had been spared at the time to make it seem so. A distinguished playgoer, Sir Henry Wotten, wrote in a letter to his nephew on the 2nd of July that 'the King's players had a new play called *All Is True*, representing some principal pieces in the reign of Henry VIII, which was set forth with many extraordinary circumstances of pomp and majesty, even to the matting of the stage . . . Now, King Henry making a masque at the Cardinal Wolsey's house, and certain chambers being shot off at his entry, some of the paper or other material wherewith one of them was stopped did light on the thatch, where being thought at first but an idle smoke, and their eyes more attentive to the show, it kindled inwardly, and ran round like a train, consuming within less than an hour the whole house to the very ground. That was the fatal period of that virtuous fabric, wherein yet nothing did perish but wood

---

4 SUFFOLK: I do assure you, the King cried Ha, at this.
CHAMBERLAIN: Now God incense him, and let him cry Ha, louder. 3.2

and straw and a few forsaken cloaks; only one had his breeches set on fire, that would have broiled him, if he had not by the benefit of a provident wit put it out with bottle ale.'

It was built all of wood, framed in a circle and roofed with thatch, and it must have burned like a furnace. Even so it is hard to believe that so large a building was all consumed 'to the very ground' in less than an hour. Another witness from the time, John Chamberlain, writing to his friend Sir Ralph Winwood, doubled the figure to 'less than two hours'. That may have been with the fire at its height and the galleries all falling into the blaze. I imagine that the wreck went on smouldering into the evening, and the smoke of it would have drifted across the river half a mile to St Paul's and Cheapside. Small crowds of people, a last audience, would have gathered at the riverside ends of the streets to watch, and the watermen would have rested on their oars to watch as they drifted by. They would have been busy all next day ferrying people across to walk around the blackened pile, still a little warm.

CHAPTER ELEVEN

EPILOGUE: A PORTRAIT
FROM LIFE

·

At the time of the fire Shakespeare was in his fiftieth year, which in those days would be considered old, as he then certainly considered himself to be. Indeed from the testimony of his second Sonnet we may suppose he had considered himself old since he was forty.[1] Living in retirement, in his fine house in Stratford, it may have been a day or two before news of the Globe's destruction would have reached him; and then despite his age, it is likely he may have girded himself to travel once again the long familiar road to London to meet with his old friends and partners, Cuthbert and Richard Burbage, to discuss possible plans for a new building. The Burbages were still living in Shoreditch where, thirty-seven years before, their father had erected the first of all the public playhouses, the Theatre, whose timbers had later gone into creation of the Globe, and now lay as a heap of black wreckage upon Bankside. A new building would therefore now have to be created with new timbers, though the site, size and foundations of the old were still in place, and there would have been no need to alter any of these.

For our own reference we have two principal contemporary engraved pictures of the Globe, one from before the fire, and one of the new building after it. Both are incidental details in panoramic views of old London, and both were drawn at dates actually subsequent to the fire. The earlier of the two (see fig. 4) was published in Amsterdam in 1616, from the studio/workshop of the engraver J. C. Visscher. Amsterdam, with Antwerp and the

---

1 'When forty winters shall besiege thy brow / And dig deep trenches in thy beauty's field, / Thy youth's proud livery, so gazed on now / Will be a tottered weed, of small worth held.'

whole region of the Lower Rhine was at that time the centre for a prolific industry of illustrative engraving which served the printing and publishing trade of all north-west Europe. It is unlikely that Visscher had ever set eyes on the Globe itself. He would have worked from sketches, some possibly drawn only from memory, supplemented by the verbal reports of visitors from London. With that concession Visscher's picture was for general purposes and for his time as good as it needed to be. He shows us a three-storeyed, many-sided building, which he evidently assumed to be octagonal, with an (ill-defined) arrangement of little huts standing out of its unroofed arena, surmounted by a flag. To demonstrate its importance as a public building he emphasised its height rather than its width, thus making a sort of fortress tower out of it, and with this it acquired for itself a romantic quality which captured the imagination of the earlier Globe reconstructionists. Moreover, belonging by chance to the date 1616, Visscher's picture can just be associated with the dates of Shakespeare's lifetime, and so directly with the dramatist's legend, which gives it a certain sentimental advantage over its rival, which dates from thirty years later. That rival picture is not, as Visscher's was, a composition made largely at second hand from the reported observations of travellers, but a direct portrait of the building, from a drawing made on site by an accomplished and reliable topographical artist, Wenceslas Hollar. Hollar had been brought to London in 1637 by Thomas Howard, Earl of Arundel, who had been James I's ambassador to the Palatinate in central Europe. The Earl possessed a great collection of ancient sculptures and other works of art (which in a later age helped to furnish the original galleries of the British Museum), and he took the young Hollar into his service partly with the idea of having him make a pictorial record of his collections. Along with this, while he was living at Arundel House in the Strand, Hollar produced his remarkable Long View of London, in the foreground of which, in the Bankside section, the Globe playhouse is clearly featured. It is an exterior view full of circumstantial detail, but of a building so unusual, and so lacking in any of the expected Tudorish picturesqueness, that earlier scholars of the subject gave it either little notice or no credence. Many did not mention it at all. Moreover the matter was not helped by Hollar himself, who having so

58 Enlargement of detail from W. Hollar's panorama drawing of Bankside, *c.* 1643. The second Globe Playhouse, drawn 'from life' from the tower of St Mary Overy's church, Southwark.

59 Hollar's Long View of London, western section.

174

carefully drawn the two neighbouring amphitheatres, the Globe and the Hope (which latter he calls the 'Beere bayting') then mistakenly reversed their names. He had taken the site drawings with him to Antwerp during the English Civil War, and it was there that he etched his Long View plates: but on his drawings the theatres are not named, and for the engraving he misremembered them.

Two only of his Long View site drawings remain – those of the extreme ends of the long set, left and right, and by good fortune the one on the left or western side shows the theatres. The drawing was made in two stages, first an overall general layout in pencil to put everything in position, and then upon that a clarifying definition of it in pen and ink. The drawing itself[2] shows a whole view over the western part of Bankside, as Hollar saw it from a position on the tower of the church of St Mary Overies, which is now Southwark Cathedral, and Globe playhouse is only a small detail in it, measuring no more than 23mm across, but we can see in a photographic enlargement of it (fig. 58) the care which Hollar had taken to present an accurate image, together with his quick compensation for a small mistake on the right-hand side of the double-gabled superstructure. In his drawing of this Hollar had slightly raised the line of the roof-ridge, so as to separate his pen line clearly from the ridge of its neighbouring left gable; but in separating the two lines he created another difficulty, for, in order to keep the pitch of the roof at its correct angle he had then slightly to enlarge the width of the right-hand gable; and so (one thing leading to another) in order to keep the relative proportions of the whole building visually correct, he ended by having to extend the overall width of it by a small amount, perhaps two or three feet in real terms. Such a correction does not discredit the values of Hollar's drawing as evidence, but rather certifies his care even in this small detail, for visual accuracy. Only in one particular of his drawing is a proportionate part of the building not clear. On neither side of it can we judge the height of the outside walls, because their footing all around is hidden from view by a surrounding of small trees or shrubs.

2 The original is in the Mellon Collection of English Drawings and Watercolours at
   Yale University.

I have in another study[3] estimated the dimensions of Hollar's Globe playhouse as shown in this drawing, as being 92-feet wide overall (excluding the staircase towers), by an (estimated) 31-feet high to the eaves, plus another 17 feet to the ridges of the two superstructure roofs: an overall total of 56 feet high, without counting the 'turret' between the twin superstructure roofs. About that turret I have here to admit a previous mistake. In my book referred to above, I described the turret as being a lantern of windows, erected to give additional light to the stage below. I am now sure that was not their purpose. The double-gabled roof had been built in that form so that the framing timbers of its twin gables, clenched together with interlocking joints at the centre, would give the greatest possible stability for its wide span over the stage. If it had been built up to a single ridge it would have been very high and very heavy at the centre, producing an impossible thrust of weight against the outer walls of the main building, which would not be able to stand against it.[4] The twin-roofed form overcomes this difficulty, but produces another, for the valley between the roof takes away the headroom within the loft which is needed for the overhead winding-gear which lets down the throne of the gods from the ornamentally-painted ceiling of the Heavens to the stage of the world below. It had therefore become necessary to build a separate loft across the central valley, especially to contain that machinery. Its position, as shown in Hollar's drawing, would lower the throne into exactly the best place, an area centred nicely in front of the tiring-house frontage, yet not too near it, and not too far forward on the stage.

I have spent these last pages in the measured examination of a very small drawing – in the original, the playhouse building is less than one inch across – because I have wished to establish its unique authority as evidence for the structural appearance of the Globe as Shakespeare knew it. If Wenzel Hollar

---

3 *Shakespeare's Second Globe*: Oxford University Press, 1973.

4 Nevertheless, in the now familiar reconstruction of the first Globe playhouse erected on Bankside in 1997, the superstructure there has been built as a single wide gable spanning the yard with its roof pitched at a shallower angle than the surrounding galleries, to reduce its height and weight. This appears generally satisfactory, though the loss of the character shown in Hollar's historic drawing may be considered disappointing.

had not made this sketch, and later his etching from it, it is as certain as can be that nobody would ever have imagined the appearance of that famous playhouse in this form. We should have had to provide a picture of it mostly from the imagination, which would probably in this case have been less unusual than imagination is usually supposed to be. The reality is in fact something very far from usual. Hollar's drawing shows us in precise terms what was in every way one of the most exceptional buildings in theatre history. The drawing and Hollar's later version of it in his etching are given together on p. 174. I will end by showing, as a tailpiece, my imagined view of how the interior of the Globe Playhouse, as rebuilt after the fire of 1613, might look if it were now to be reconstructed as faithfully as possible for modern use.

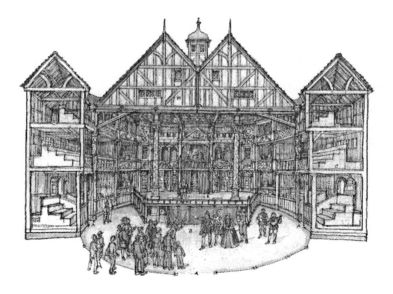

177

INDEX

Printed in the United Kingdom
by Lightning Source UK Ltd.
105076UKS00002B/195-196